1 MONTH OF
FREE
READING

at
www.ForgottenBooks.com

By purchasing this book you are eligible for one month membership to ForgottenBooks.com, giving you unlimited access to our entire collection of over 1,000,000 titles via our web site and mobile apps.

To claim your free month visit:
www.forgottenbooks.com/free424894

* Offer is valid for 45 days from date of purchase. Terms and conditions apply.

ISBN 978-0-265-36059-0
PIBN 10424894

Note

upon

"Dark Lady" Series

of

Shakspeare's Sonnets

By

John K. Strong

But yet there is a credence in my heart,
An esperance so obstinately strong,
That doth invert the attest of eyes and ears;
As if those organs had deceptious functions,
Created only to calumniate.

Troilus and Cressida, V. ii. 120.

Illustrated

G. P. Putnam's Sons
New York and London

Note

upon

The "Dark Lady" Series

of

Shakspeare's Sonnets

By

John R. Strong

Sith yet there is a credence in my heart,
An esperance so obstinately strong,
That doth invert the attest of eyes and ears;
As if those organs had deceptious functions,
Created only to calumniate.

Troilus and Cressida, V, ii, 120.

Illustrated

G. P. Putnam's Sons
· New York and London
The Knickerbocker Press
1921

Printed in the United States of America

CONTENTS

ILLUSTRATIONS

NOTE UPON
SHAKSPEARE'S SONNETS
CXXVII–CLII

THE PUBLICATION OF THE SONNETS

THE leading question as to Shakspeare's sonnets to the "Dark Lady" is the question of their history, for it necessarily involves and is a key to most of the other questions which arise in reading the sonnets, and, besides, on its answer many questions of wider interest in Shakspeare's life and dramatic work may perhaps depend. The object of this Note is to review the most probable theory of the history of these sonnets, and to see how far it can bring us toward any firm knowledge as to this striking incident in the poet's career.

It is not likely that the poet intended that these sonnets should be made public; that two of the twenty-five or twenty-six sonnets (CXXXVIII, CXLIV) of the "Dark Lady" series were published in *The Passionate Pilgrim* in 1599 should be ascribed, of course, to accident. The two straying sonnets were perhaps mislaid, perhaps misappropriated draughts, not only because they differed materially from the ten-years-later text of the general Quarto of the sonnets, but also because the three other

Shakspearean pieces pirated with them not only differed considerably from their standard text, but were pirated and published in the year after that standard text had appeared in the Quarto of *Love's Labour's Lost* of 1598. Shakspeare's offense at the publication of *The Passionate Pilgrim*, in which the two strayed sketches, or early forms, from the "Dark Lady" series appeared, is mentioned by Thomas Heywood, in his *Apology for Actors*, in 1612, but just a little equivocally, as if intending by coupling Shakspeare's resentment with his own resentment at a piracy committed against himself in the third edition of *The Passionate Pilgrim*, published also in 1612, to convey the impression to the reader that Shakspeare's annoyance was at that edition particularly. His words are, and the great respect shown in them for Shakspeare—it was then only four years before the dramatist's decease— should be especially noticed:

Here, likewise, I must necessarily insert a manifest injury done to me in that worke [*his "Troia Brittanica," 1609*], by taking the two epistles of Paris to Helen, and Helen to Paris, and printing them in a lesse volume, [*the third edition of "The Passionate Pilgrim," 1612*], under the name of another [*Shakspeare*], which may put the world in opinion I might steale them from him [*Shakspeare*], and hee, to doe himselfe right, hath since published them in his owne name: but, as I must acknowledge my lines not worthy his [*Shakspeare's*] patronage under whom he [*the publisher, Jaggard*] hath publisht them, so the author I know much offended with M. Jaggard (that altogether unknowne to him) presumed to make so bold with his name.

Among the numerous piracies of Shakspeare's work and misuses of his name, this is the single record of his notice of any of them, and no particular ground for offense appears in this instance of a common indifference to literary rights, excepting the publication of these unquestionably private sonnets, and on the first two pages of the Miscellany. There is sufficient reason in the sonnets themselves to account for his annoyance at this publication, while there is nothing whatever in the book besides, we may say with confidence, at which he could have been so "much offended" by it. What else was there in it which could cause an author of his experience in plagiarism to pay any attention to it, except these two sonnets? His annoyance must have occurred, however, before the edition of 1612. Shakspeare, in 1612, was not at a time of life when he would much trouble himself about any such publication, and besides, no appearance of the sonnets could, at that time, have so much annoyed him, as the Quarto of all the

sonnets had been published three years before, in
1609, including the two in question. Certainly,
the poet could have cared nothing about the addition to Jaggard's Miscellany of Heywood's work,
the Paris-Helen letters, an idle work added to
others which were worse. His displeasure therefore, if it was expressed at all by him in 1612, and
if Heywood's report of it was not merely an application to the moment of words which he had heard,
or heard of, long before, could not have been more
than a mere allusion to a past vexation, a vexation
felt at the first edition of *The Passionate Pilgrim*
in 1599, and again at the second edition, for their
publication of these most personal and private
sonnets. The closeness with which Shakspeare's
sonnets were kept to his friends is remarkable,
especially when their literary merit and personal
interest are considered; none of those in the Quarto
of 1609 appeared earlier in any publication, except
the two printed in *The Passionate Pilgrim*. Sonnet CXLIV, besides its intimate character, contains introspective elements, in an unusual imagery
and in a noteworthy disclosure of spiritual conflict,
the unscrupulous publication of which he might
regard as an infraction of all literary comity and
good will. On the other sonnet it is unnecessary to
remark, save that it appears to give a slight indi-

cation of who the lady was. The time of publication may perhaps have coincided, as will be seen in the course of this Note, with his anxiety and distress in respect to the lady involved. The title of the book, and the ascription of the book to him as its author, would, under the circumstances, probably not diminish his annoyance. The belief then appears to be not without an apparent foundation, through Heywood's evidence as to Shakspeare's displeasure, as well as through the intrinsic probability arising from the character of the sonnets, and, of course, through Shakspeare's practice, who seldom published at all, that the sonnets of the "Dark Lady" series would not have been given to publication by their author.

MARY FYTTON

The first sonnet in the series, which is a singularly beautiful one, is almost certainly founded upon the following passage in *Love's Labour's Lost:*

O, if in black my lady's brows be decked,
   It *mourns* that painting and usurping hair

Should ravish doters with a false aspect;
  And therefore is she born to make black fair.
Her favour turns the fashion of the days,
  For native blood is counted painting now;
And therefore red, that would avoid dispraise,
  Paints itself black, to imitate her brow.

             Love's Labour's Lost, IV, iii, 258.

The later, or more probably coincident, sonnet is:

In the old age black was not counted fair,
Or if it were, it bore not beauty's name;
But now is black beauty's successive heir,
And beauty slandered with a bastard shame:
For since each hand hath put on nature's power,
Fairing the foul with art's false borrowed face,
Sweet beauty hath no name, no holy bower,
But is profaned, if not lives in disgrace.
Therefore my mistress' eyes are raven black,
Her eyes so suited, and they *mourners* seem
At such who, not born fair, no beauty lack,
Slandering creation with a false esteem.
  Yet so they *mourn*, becoming of their woe,
  That every tongue says beauty should look so.

                Sonnet CXXVII.

The argument of the sonnet appears to be that fairness of complexion is shamed by the habit of painting plain faces fair, and that dark beauty, therefore, becoming the successor in esteem of fairness of face, seems to *mourn* at the imitators of fair

complexion. This is also the argument of the
passage from the play, maintained through the
sonnet notwithstanding the changes made in re-
writing. Each is based on the contrast between
black and fair, and each gives the same reason for
advancing the claims of dark beauty, that fair
beauty is discredited. Neither, notwithstanding
its praise of dark beauty, contains an expression of
preference for dark beauty over fair. In the word
mourn, the keynote is struck of the description of
the lady in each, and the word in Sonnet CXXXII
is used still oftener. Sonnet CXXVII does not
include the last, extreme statement of the passage,
that fair faces made themselves darker to follow
the newer fashion, that compliment, allowed by the
speaker's enthusiasm, being perhaps replaced, with
less extravagance, by the fine couplet of the sonnet.
In line 11 of the sonnet are the words "beauty
lack," which occur in the play a few lines before
the passage cited. Rosaline's eyes—the passage is
a part of a description of Rosaline—are compli-
mented at nearly the same point in the play, and
again, earlier in the scene, at lines 10 and 243, while
the eyes of the lady of the sonnet are also especially
referred to, and again in CXXXII, CXXXIX,
CXLIX, and in other sonnets.

The conclusion seems irresistible, when the sonnet and the passage are read together, the arguments and their treatment being essentially the same, that Shakspeare wrote the sonnet from, or at the same time with, the passage, and it is certain that he addressed the sonnet to a lady whom he could describe in the same terms as those which are used in the play. There can be no reason to hesitate as to the substantial identity of the sonnet and the passage, nor as to the resemblance of the ladies mentioned, and there is substantial reason, therefore, for the inquiry whether there is any further connection between the sonnet and the play. We may then ask: Was the passage in the play descriptive, as was the sonnet, of a particular person? And, if that appears to be maintainable, or probable, or at least possible, we may also ask: Were the two persons described the same lady?

Love's Labour's Lost was published in 1598 as newly revised, and as it had been performed at the Court in the preceding Christmas season. The character of Rosaline appears in the play as distinctly as if it were a copy from some lady who was well known to the poet, and shows a personal touch in the portraiture. It differs from those of the other ladies in the play, the Princess of France, Maria and Katherine, in that it is less of an abstract idea, or of a stage conception, and more of

a complex, yet single, individuality, differing from
those ladies more than they differ from each other,
and seeming rather like a pen-portrait of a living
original than a creation of fancy. The personal
quality in her lines seems as if it were exactly that
which comes from the representation on the stage
of some one whose personal character is known to
the playwright. There are also in her delineation
incidents which seem to spring from such a knowledge by the poet. Her vanquishing Katherine in
two skirmishes, once about her character, and
again over her dark beauty, much strengthens the
theory that a private history is shadowed in the
play, as, of course, is some general history (V,
ii, 19, 42). Her characteristic "It is not so," is
repeated as though the poet had heard the words,
and remembered them as a type of her rapid comprehension. (V, ii, 188, 364, 426.) Very marked
is the scene in which he places her in the chair of
royalty, to receive the Russian visitors, and her
words, while so seated, seem echoes of a known
voice rather than the phrases of his imagination
only. (V, ii, 174.) Nowhere, in all Shakspeare's
characterizations of ladies, is there another such
presentation of womanly alertness of mind, coupled
with an attractive despotism, unless in his later
portrait of Cleopatra, and even that is not so

simply and directly the life itself. The poet seems
also, perhaps, though this depends even more
upon a reader's interpretation, to have attributed
his own style in writing to the talk of Rosaline's
lover, in the line:

> So sweet and voluble is his discourse.
>> *Love's Labour's Lost, II, i, 76.*

Such unsubstantial appeals to the imagination
only as the preceding cannot carry proof, but they
may go so far, as in this case, which is perhaps
enforced a little beyond strict warrant, as to show
that there is reason for an interesting speculation,
and a possibility worth considering, that there was
a living original for Rosaline. With a basis, then,
for imagining the sonnet to have had a connection
of some kind with the revision of the play, and
some little ground for thinking that Rosaline represented some one living, as must have the sonnet,
and further, it being certain that the two representations of women are of persons of much the
same appearance and—and this is the principal
coincidence—of questioned character, and then,
there being a very possible coincidence in time
between the revision of the play in 1597 and the
writing of the sonnet, which was certainly earlier
than 1599—that is, before the publication of the

two later sonnets of the series in *The Passionate Pilgrim* in 1599, the likeness of the sonnet to the passage from the play in itself suggesting a like time of composition—it seems to be a possible inference that the two indistinct and shadowy ladies represented in the play and in the sonnet may have been the same person. The remarkable speech of ardent homage to Rosaline, of which the passage cited is a part, and the comments upon it of a rather exceptional vivacity, should belong to the revision, and not to the much-too-early first draught of the play, which partly remains here and there in the text; a comparison of this description of Rosaline with the clearly earlier parts of the play will indicate that it belongs to the revision beyond any doubt. (IV, iii, 221; and compare the earlier I, i, 1 *et seq.*; I, i, 100, *et seq.;* I, i, 200, *et seq.*)

The similarity between the passage from the play and the sonnet, and the likeness in person and character of the ladies described, and also the possibility or probability of an identical time of writing for the revision of the play and the sonnet, do not constitute direct proof that they refer to the same person, still less that they both refer to a living person, but this result is less clear if this evidence is read with the indirect evidence as to the possible or probable origin of both the sonnet and the play. While not sufficient for proof, there is in these coincidences of text and time and personal description enough to give a definite, although a still imperfect support to a theory of a double portraiture by the poet, in the sonnet and in *Love's Labour's Lost*, of the same lady.

An explanation of these remarkable coincidences of character and complexion, that the resemblance of the sonnet to the play arose from a common portraiture of the much-discussed Mary Fytton, is one for which the evidence is a tissue of probabilities, there being no certainty for or against the suggestion. The young lady came to the Court in or near 1595 as one among the Maids of Honour to Queen Elizabeth, and at the outset of 1601, and a little over three years after the performance of *Love's Labour's Lost* at the Court, it was known that she had been misled in the preceding year by the eldest son of the Earl of Pembroke, Lord Herbert, and she had his refusal to marry her, a positive refusal, he receiving a term of imprisonment and the Queen's lasting displeasure. She therefore was at the Court in 1597, the year of *Love's Labour's Lost*, then nineteen years old, and certainly one of the leaders, or of the prospective leaders, among the Maids of Honor; she might then have been sketched among the ladies of the Court of the Princess of France by Shakspeare. Rosaline's character in the play is sketched as questionable, notwithstanding her brightness of intellect, thus resembling the character of Mary Fytton. (III, i, 200; IV, iii, 3; V, ii, 20.) It will be seen in the first letter introduced towards the end of this Note from the correspondence of Sir William Knollys, a letter written early in 1598, that Mary Fytton's reputation at the Court was, at that time probably much that which is described as Rosaline's in the revision of the play in 1597, and also that which is ascribed in the sonnets to the "Dark Lady." This is not so with the other attendants on the Princess of France, and as the imputation is unnecessary for the purposes of the play, an intrusion upon its natural order, and wholly exceptional among Shakspeare's heroines, it is a point worth much attention. Doubtless he intended to draw a "light" attendant on, or Maid of Honor of, the Princess of France, but that he should have done so is altogether unusual in his plays, and raises a question as to his motive. The balance of evidence inclines, reviewing what little can now be ascertained of this almost forgotten chapter in Elizabethan Court history, to the theory that this Maid of Honor was the "Dark Lady," the probabilities inclining to that effect proceeding from her situation at Court and her later life, the comparison of dates, the element of evidence in *Love's Labour's Lost,* and some words of the sonnets, of *All's Well that Ends Well*, of *Hamlet*, and of *Measure for Measure*, while the unconvincing nature of considerations which have been thought to counterbalance these probabilities is possibly more or less demonstrable. It may interest the reader to trace her career, and judge of her character, in some detail.

Mary Fytton's prominence in the Court circle (we can still see that the young Earl of Rutland in 1598 sent his portrait by Robert Peake to her, according to the Duke of Rutland's MSS., vol. IV, p. 418, *Historical MSS. Com.*, and verses seem to have been written to her), her favour with the Queen, and her quickness of wit, in certainly one instance, in replying to the Queen "Affection," when asked who she was as a Muse, resemble the representation of Rosaline as an attendant upon the Princess of France, and if Rosaline had a relation to the "Dark Lady" of the sonnets, resemble that misty lady also. These elements of prominence, nearness to the Queen, and readiness in reply, appear in a cotemporary series of letters describing a Masque at Court on June 16, 1600, at the marriage of a

Maid of Honor, Mistress Anne Russell, a brilliant and triumphant scene for Mary Fytton at first, and close on the time of her fatal misstep. The writer of the letters was Mr. Rowland Whyte, news-gatherer and Court representative for Lord Herbert's maternal uncle, Sir Robert Sidney, who was a brother of the deceased Sir Philip Sidney; Sir Robert was then absent from England as Lord Governor of Flushing. The letters appear in *The Sidney Papers*, transcribed from original letters at Penshurst, and as they present an interesting picture of the time, we will quote them somewhat freely:

The marriage between the other Lord Harbert [This Lord Herbert was the Earl of Worcester's son, not the Earl of Pembroke's], and Mrs. Anne Russell, is at a Stay, till yt please her Majestie to apoint a Day. . . . The Feast wilbe in Blackfriers, my Lady Russell making exceeding preparacions for yt.

Baynard's Castell, May 16, 1600.

Mrs. Anne Russell went from Court upon Monday last, with 18 Coaches, the like hath not bene seen amongest the Maydes. The Queen in publiq, used of her as gracious Speaches, as have bene hard of any, and comanded all the Mayds to accompany her to London; soe did all the Lords of the Court. Her Mother brought a great Nomber of Strangers to Court; all went in a Troope away. The Marriage wilbe upon Monday next, her Majestie wilbe there, as it is hoped.

Baynard's Castell, June 11, 1600.

Her Majesty is in very good Health, and purposes to honor Mrs. Anne Russell's Marriage with her Presence. . . . There is to be a memorable Maske of 8 Ladies; they have a straunge Dawnce newly invented; their attire is this: Each hath a Skirt of Cloth of Silver, a rich Wastcoat wrought with Silkes, and Gold and Silver, a Mantell of Carnacion Taffete cast under the Arme, and there Haire loose about their Shoulders, curiously knotted and interlaced. These are the Maskers. My Lady Doritye, Mrs. Fitton, Mrs. Carey, Mrs. Onslow, Mrs. Southwell, Mrs. Bes. Russell, Mrs. Darcy, and my Lady Blanche Somersett. These 8 dawnce to the Musiq Apollo bringes, and there is a fine Speach that makes mention of a Ninth [no doubt, the bride], much to her Honor and Praise. The preparacion for this Feast is sumptuous and great. but it is feared, that the Howse in Blackfriars wilbe to litle for such a Company.

Greenwich, June 14, 1600.

This day senight her Majestie was at Blackfriars, to grace the Marriage of the Lord Harbert and his Wiffe. The Bride mett the Queen at the Waterside, where my Lord Cobham had provided a Lectica, made like half a Litter, wherein she was carried to my Lady Russel's by 6 Knights. Her Majestie dined there, and, at Night, went thorough Dr. Puddin's Howse (who gave the Queen a Fanne) to my Lord Cobham's, where she supt. After Supper the Maske came in, as I writ in my last; and delicate it was to see 8 Ladies soe pretily and richly attired. Mrs. Fitton leade, and after they had donne all their owne Ceremonies, these 8 Ladys Maskers choose 8 Ladies more to dawnce the

Measures. Mrs. Fitton went to the Queen, and woed her to dawnce; her Majestie asked what she was; Affection, she said. Affection! said the Queen, Affection is false. Yet her Majestie rose and dawnced; soe did my Lady Marques [of Winchester].

At Court, June 23, 1600.

The remark of the old Queen's, reported by Mr. Whyte, who was evidently present, seems to have been a personal rebuke to her brilliant Maid of Honour, in view, perhaps, of the latter's already certainly questioned behaviour, but was softened by her Majesty's rising and joining in the dance. Mr. Whyte's minute account of the incident perhaps indicates Mary's prominence, and also its interest to Sir Robert Sidney. The Earl of Pembroke's son, Lord Herbert, with Lord Cobham, it is said, conducted the bride to the church for the wedding ceremony. Another allusion to this "great marriage" occurs in John Chamberlain's Letters, mentioning the Masque as "in name of the Muses that came to seeke one of their fellowes."

There are some other letters, interesting on the general question, and giving each a light of its own, some taken from Lady Newdegate's collection of the letters of the Fytton family, the invaluable *Gossip from a Muniment Room*, and some occurring elsewhere. In a letter dated July 3,

1598, Mary's mother, Lady Fytton, writing to her elder daughter, Mrs. Anne Newdigate, seems to have thought that Mary had become deficient in attention to her, for she says: "If you heer any thynge of your sister I pray you let know, for I nevar harde ffrom herr synce." In that year Lord Herbert, aged eighteen, first came to the Court as a member of it, but probably not in the spring, as has been suggested, but "some few days" after June 18th. (Pembroke to Cecil, *Hist. MSS. Com.*, Salisbury MSS., Part 8, p. 219.) Mary's inattention, then, communication by letter being generally slow at the time, was probably not at all connected with Lord Herbert's arrival. The letters in the Arbury collection are said to have been "invariably sent by hand." There is but one brief note from Mary known to the editor of the Fytton Letters; it is undated and written in "a scrawling hand," as Lady Newdegate tells us, to her sister, Anne, perhaps the most animated, perhaps it may be said, excited, note in the book:

To my dearest syster, Mris An. Newdigate. Since distance bares me from so gret hapenes as I can seldom hear from you, which when I do is so welcome, as I esteme nothing more worthie, and for your love, which I dout not of, shal be equeled in ful mesuer, but lest my lines to tedius wear, and time that limetes all thinges bares me of wordes, which eles could never ses

to tel howe dear you ar, and with what sele I desire
your retourne, than can wish nothing then your hartes
desir, and wil ever continou Your afectionet sister,

MARY PHYTTON.

The rapidity, brevity, emotional excitement and
enforcement of her love for her sister, which can be
read in this note, are its striking characteristics,
and perhaps account for its preservation by her
sister. The reference to the limitation of time is in
a noticeably high style for so brief a note, certainly
resembling a little a Shakspearean echo, as far as it
goes. Her apparent tide of happiness, as well as
her wish for her sister's presence, are also worth
consideration. In themselves unnoticeable, the
words "lest my lines to tedius wear," taken in
connection with the possible reflex of conversations
with the dramatist, suggested by the reference to
time, are not unlike what might be said by a person
interested in a dramatist, and thus in dramatic and
other composition. The want of a date in this
letter makes it quite impossible to certainly place
it. From its fresh girlishness, when compared with
the increasingly trying conditions of her later years
at the Court, as will appear further in this essay,
the tendency of the reader will be to place it early
in her career there. "Ses" and "sele," mean cease
and zeal. "Retourne" might mean Anne's return

to the family's house in London, or to the Court nearby, at Nonsuch. The words "than" and "then," which follow, should, for the sake of syntax, perhaps be exchanged, one for the other. The family name appears variously in its spelling, various spelling seeming to have been the fashion; it is written Ffytton, Ffyton, Fytton, Fyton, Phytton, Phyton, Phitton, Fiton, Fitten and, perhaps most usually, Fitton. Her parents appear to have always signed Ffytton or Ffyton. In this essay, the spelling Fytton is adopted.

What else of her life, during her stay at Court, is to be recorded here, will be found in the correspondence of Sir William Knollys, in remarks upon the course of events leading to Mary's fall and upon her character, and upon her illness in 1600, in a reference to her patronage of the actor, William Kempe, and in the elucidations of sonnets whose allusions may be connected with her. We continue with her history after the Russell wedding.

In the Calendar of the Carew MSS., is a letter from Sir Robert Cecil to Sir George Carew, dated at Court, February 5, 1601. A postscript to this letter—the letter refers to Sir George Carew's Governorship of the Province of Munster—is interesting as a confirmation from almost the highest source of the Herbert-Fytton story:

P. S.   We have no news but that there is a misfortune befallen Mistress Fitton, for she is proved with child, and the Earl of Penbrooke, being examined, confesseth a fact, but utterly renounceth all marriage. I fear they will both dwell in the Tower awhile, for the Queen hath vowed to send them thither.

Lord Herbert is called the Earl of Pembroke because his father, who was ill beyond prospect of recovery at the time of this exposure, died January 19, 1601. The letter is preceded in the Carew MSS. by one from Sir John Stanhope to Sir George Carew, dated "this 26 of January," meaning in 1601, saying:

Of the persecution which is like to befall the poor maids' chamber in Court, and of Fytton's afflictions, and lastly her commitment to my Lady Hawkyns, of the discouragement thereby of the rest, though it be now out of your element to think of, yet I doubt not but that some friend doth more particularly advertise you.

In the Public Record Office is a letter from "pretty, little" Toby Matthew to Dudley Carleton containing this item, and dated March 25, 1601:

The Earl of Pembroke is committed to the Fleet: his cause is delivered of a boy, who is dead.

Mary was taken home then by her father to Gawsworth. Sir Edward Fytton, Mary's father, wrote to Sir Robert Cecil as follows: (Calendar of the Salisbury MSS., Part II):

Here-enclosed are divers examinations sent to me as Mayor of Maxfeld [Macclesfield], and come to me at Stamer [Stanmore], in the night, where I was enforced to abide by reason of my daughter's weakness.
. . . I say nothing of the Earl [of Pembroke], but my daughter is confident in her claim before God, and wishes my Lord and she might but meet before indifferent hearers. But for myself, I expect no good from him, that in all this time has not shewed any kindness. I count my daughter as good a gentlewoman as my Lord, though the dignity of honour be greater only in him, which has beguiled her I fear, except my Lord's honesty be the greater virtues.

18 May [1601], at Stanmer.

Lord Herbert's attitude in the matter was that not only a particular but a general assault had been made to the Queen upon his character, and that, in the latter respect, he was innocent. He writes to Sir Robert Cecil, from Wilton House, the residence of his father, who was then dying, as follows; the letters are in the Marquis of Salisbury's Calendar of Manuscripts (*Hist. MSS. Com.*, Part II):

You have given me so many testimonies of your love, that I will plainly and absolutely put myself into your hands. I was sent to by a very friend of

mine to come post to the Court, and not to fail of
being there to wait on Tuesday at dinner, if I would
not utterly lose the Queen's favour: a sentence of little
more comfort than hanging: and yet if I had made all
the haste I could, I should hardly have been there by
the time, receiving the letters but this Monday morning about 8 o'clock: and if I could perchance have
been there by the time, I leave to your judgment how
fit to wait that day. Therefore, if ever you will express your love, let me find it in this, for if I cannot
obtain her Majesty's favour to remain with my Lord
[his father] in his weakness, I shall quite overthrow my
fortune. . . . I beseech you bestow a few lines in
post upon me that I may know my doom.

Wilton, Monday morning at 10 o'clock.
Endorsed by Sir Robert, *5 Jan. 1601, Lord Herbert.*

There hath been many false and scandalous reports
forged of me, which have as maliciously been delivered
unto her Majesty, to make her, if it were possible, to
withdraw her former favour from me: taking this
advantage of my absence when I could make no answer
for myself, but I doubt not in the end the shame will
fall upon themselves. Yet they have driven me to this
inconvenience, that when I should sue for a benefit I
am forced to excuse a fault, two actions unfit to be
coupled together, but as my state now is, not to be
divided. You know there be some offices now fallen
into the Queen's hands which my Lord in his life-time
held, and though of small commodity, yet the disgrace of not being as worthy as another to enjoy them
after him will be to me exceeding great. Therefore I
beseech you thus much to stand my friend, that they

may be stayed till I have the happiness to speak with her Majesty myself.

Wilton, this 18 of January in the evening. (*1601.*)
P. S. If you have not a note of the offices, Rowland White shall deliver one unto you.

After these letters, the young Earl seems to have spent some time in the Fleet prison, and on his emergence wrote to Sir Robert Cecil, as follows:

The imposition you laid upon me for my wardship [the interval between the old Earl's decease and the new Earl's coming of age], though it be a very heavy burden on my weak means, having so many great payments to make besides; yet since it is her Majesty's pleasure, I will not dispute it, but wholly submit myself to her sacred will. I think myself much favoured by her Majesty, that it would please her to give me leave to go abroad to follow my own business: but I cannot forbear telling of you that yet I endure a very grievous imprisonment. . . . In this vile case am I, whose miserable fortune it is to be banished from the sight of her [the Queen], in whose favour the balance consisted of my misery or happiness, and whose incomparable beauty was the only sun of my little world, that alone had power to give it light and heat. Now judge you whether this be a bondage or no.

Baynard's Castle, 19 June.
Endorsed, *1601, Earl of Pembroke.*

I have not yet been a day in the country, and I am as weary of it as if I had been a prisoner there seven years. I see I shall never turn good Justice of the

Peace. Therefore I pray, if the Queen determine to continue my banishment, and prefer sweet Sir Edward [Fytton?] before me, that you will assist me with your best means to get leave to go into some other land, that the change of the climate may purge me of melancholy: for else I shall never be fit for any civil society. I have written, sorrowfully complaining, to my Lord Admiral that he will be pleased to move my suit again, since there is no appearance of grace. The patent of the Forest of Dean could not so speedily be gotten before my going out of town, but very shortly Arthur Massinger shall attend you with it.

Undated: endorsed, 13 Aug. 1601.

What love and thankfulness you could have expected from me if I had prevailed, the same to the best of my power you shall find me ready to perform on all occasions, now that I am disgraced. Her Majesty, as I heard, when she promised Mr. Mumpersons a Park, after my Lord your father's death, when she knew how nearly it concerned my Lord Burghley in honour, recalled her promise, preserved my Lord's honour, and graciously satisfied her servant another way. If it had pleased her Majesty as graciously to have conceived in this matter of the Forest of Dean, of that poor reputation I was desirous to preserve, the maintenance whereof might have enabled [me] to do her Majesty more honour and service than now I am able to perform, I should have been happy, and Sir Edward [Winter?] might another way as well have been satisfied. But since her Majesty has in her wisdom thought fit to lay this disgrace upon me, I accuse nothing but my own unworthiness, which since I so plainly read in my own fortunes, I will alter my hopes, and teach them to propose unto themselves no other ends than such as they shall be sure to receive no disgrace in. The hawk that is once canvast will the next time take heed of the net; and shall I that was born a man and capable of reason, commit greater folly than birds that have naught but sense to direct them? If her Majesty make this the returning way for her favour, though it be like the way of salvation, narrow and crooked, yet my hopes dare not travel through the ruggedness of it, for they stumble so often that before they come half way they despair of passing such difficulties. There be some things yet in her Majesty's hands to dispose of, which if it would please her to grace me with, might happely [sic] in some measure patch up my disgrace in the opinion of the world. But I have vowed never again to be a suitor, since in my first suit I have received such a blow.

Ramsbury, 2 Sept., (1601).

Yesternight I received a message from my Lord Admiral by my uncle, that, when his Lordship moved the Queen for me, she said she would have me go keep house in the country. How unfit this course will be for me, I am sure you are sufficiently satisfied. Only this I have gotten, that I perceive her Majesty still continues in her wonted displeasure towards me, for when she was in the height of her anger, her answer was the very same. I request that all motions for me but for my travel may not so much as be remembered. When I last spoke with you, you made no doubt of obtaining my leave. I beseech you still be earnest in it.

Undated: ascribed to Oct., 1601.

I know not how to be sufficiently thankful for so great a favour bestowed on me, in getting the Queen to consent for my going beyond the seas, but you may assure yourself that while I live I will ever remain wholly devoted to do you service. I beseech you, while her Majesty is in this good disposition, you will give order to Mr. Lake to draw my license, and procure her Majesty's gracious hand, and then you shall be delivered from an importunate suitor that often troubled you with many idle businesses.

Undated: endorsed, *Earl of Pembroke, 1601.*

There are an insensibility and a presumptuousness about these letters, written under circumstances so painful and discreditable, which make a poor appearance in the cold light of history, particularly Lord Herbert's general attitude toward his fault, his cool and also injudicious comparison of his claims with those of the second Lord Burghley, Sir Robert Cecil's half-brother, a man honoured, if not for himself, still in recognition of the first Lord Burghley's transcendent services (*September 2d*), and his persistent suit for office. The Queen's decision that he should "go keep house in the country" seems to have been, in the circumstances, an eminently just one. Surely this was not the man upon whom Shakspeare lavished his enthusiastic admiration in the earlier sonnets. According to Mr. Tyler, the Patent of the Forest of

Dean was returned by the young Earl, through Arthur Massinger, to Sir Robert Cecil, and was afterwards reissued, not to the Earl, but to Sir Edward Winter, who is the "Sir Edward" mentioned in the letters (*Shakespeare's Sonnets*, Tyler's Ed., p. 63), and during the remainder of the reign of the Queen, at least, the Earl lost the care of the Forest. The *Historical MSS. Commission*, in whose Report the letters are found, have thought that by "Sir Edward," Sir Edward Fytton was meant. It seems to be clear from the context that in the letter of August it is rather Sir Edward Fytton who is intended, and in that of September, Sir Edward Winter. If this is a correct understanding of the letters, and it seems to be quite plain, the allusion to Sir Edward Fytton is in the poorest taste. The remaining offices "now fallen into the Queen's hands" (letter of January 18th), appear to have been minor dignities of the family, lapsed on the death of the old Earl, a note of which Rowland Whyte was to bring to Sir Robert Cecil. Near the letters in the Salisbury Calendar (p. 99), is a list of "Stewardships of castles" and "keeping of Claringdon Park, Wilts," stated to be "offices lately in possession of Henry, Earl of Pembroke," and which may possibly be the "note of the offices" to be sent through Rowland Whyte, and for which the new Earl pleaded so insensibly and irrepressibly. If the Earl went abroad it was not for very long, as at Christmas-time, 1602, he appears in Rutlandshire passing a "royal Christmas" with his friends.

Clarendon's account of this Earl of Pembroke, in the introductory part of his History, is rather eulogistic than reliable, if we accept comprehensively his own statement of the Earl's career. Pembroke was of the generation preceding that of Clarendon, who was little more than twenty-one years old at Pembroke's death, and the portrait drawn of him by Clarendon is therefore more a summary of the eulogies of surviving friends than the impartial and just description of an eye-witness. Through his dissolute habits he became, at the last, according to Clarendon's review of him, impaired in his health, dying without issue. His yearly income is said to have been £22,000, representing four or five times as much, as money is valued now. His letters, in their cultivated style, resemble those of Lord Southampton and the other cultured men of the time, the result, in great measure, of the careful tutoring which, as we know, he must have had. A sentence of Shakspeare's, in one of his earlier plays, applies with aptness to Lord Herbert's letters (*II Hen. IV.*, II, i, 121). They point to a substantial poorness of disposition in Lord Herbert; apparent throughout, in his allusion to Sir Edward Fytton (August 13th) in his fling, a little lacking in respect in the last clause quoted, at the Queen (June 19th), and in the other uninspiring characteristics of them already mentioned.

The reasons for the belief that Shakspeare's earlier sonnets were written to Lord Southampton, and not to Lord Herbert, cannot be entered into in this essay. Lord Southampton was married to Elizabeth Vernon in 1598, after a long courtship, and one of considerable intensity, within the period therefore in which the sonnets to the "Dark Lady" were being written, as is the best inference from the date of *The Passionate Pilgrim*, 1599, and the connection with them of Lord Southampton is therefore far less likely than that of Lord Herbert. If we connect the first sonnet of the "Dark Lady" series with the year of the revision of *Love's Labour's Lost*, 1597, and the concluding sonnets of the series with *The Passionate Pilgrim*, in which two of them appeared, in 1599, we have a period of about two years, mid 1597-1599, for the composition of the "Dark Lady" series, and this is in harmony with the uniform style of the sonnets themselves.

Sonnet CXXXIV, in its doubtless accurate presentation of legal learning as to the redemption of a mortgaged estate and the obligation of a surety, was probably coincident with Shakspeare's efforts in 1597 and thereafter to relieve Asbies, his mother's property, from the tenure of John Lambert, heir of the mortgagee.

Piecing together the facts known from the acknowledged records, and adding to them some indications appearing in the sonnets, both within and without the "Dark Lady" series, we can with some probability reconstruct the course of events in the Shakspeare-Herbert-Fytton story, as follows. If we may suppose that Mary Fytton did feel an attachment for the poet, a marriage with him was, of course, quite out of the question. We have the still charming, though hasty and excited, tone of the solitary letter of hers which we possess, and which may, perchance, have been written near the commencement of the series of sonnets which we are inclined to attribute to her influence. In estimating the character of Mary Fytton at the time of her misstep and before it, we are chiefly impressed by her personal ascendency, her cleverness, her great power of attraction and her carelessness of any moral code. Her situation at the

Court was one which would become, necessarily, increasingly painful and trying. She was oppressed by the attentions of a Sir William Knollys, a cotemporary of her father's, who had undertaken to be her defender and counselor at the Court, whom she had permitted to become fascinated by her, and to whom she had granted also a species of engagement, dependent upon the death of his wife, a matrimonial prospect which there is reason to believe she disliked, and a contract also which she seems to have felt at liberty to break at any moment for one more immediate and suitable. There seem to have been rumours about the Court, whether connecting her with the poet or not we cannot now know, and which must have been painful to her as they were denied belief by Sir William. Her position thus tending to become ever more doubtful and dissatisfying, there came the high success of Mistress Anne Russell, also a Maid of Honour, with the other Lord Herbert, the Earl of Worcester's son—it was certainly near to the time of that great wedding that Mary made her fatal misstep— and beyond this incitement to her emulation, there was the Queen's open rebuke at the time, which might induce her to wish to justify herself by a corresponding success. The Court of the old Queen, as we learn from the Fytton Letters, had

weakened its minor discipline, at least in respect
to the Maids of Honour, and the young lady was
therefore much at her own disposal. Lord Herbert's instant refusal to marry her, though she was
of a distinguished family and eminently attractive,
cannot but cast a shadow of question on her, and
it is deepened by the rumours of her at the Court
as well as by her subsequent career. Some time
earlier, or so the circumstances seem to indicate,
she had felt herself compelled to place her hopes,
without delay, in some direction more suitable to
her age than Sir William, and she seems to have
increased an acquaintance into a pursuit, which
was generally noticed, of Lord Herbert, a youth
probably soon to be Earl of Pembroke, who was a
newcomer at the Court, and who, though of an
early maturity, as his letters show, was nearly two
years younger than herself. That she should have
tolerated or permitted the familiarities of the
irresponsible young man, the future Earl, having
especial reason for caution with him, as he might
suspect her of imprudence with the poet (Sonnets
CXXXIII, CXXXIV), was a part of the error
which is inseparable from a nature such as hers.
Relying on her own powers, and more and more
involved in her pursuit, she might imagine that at
the price of some freedom with the most powerful

of her suitors, she could, through persuading him
to ask for marriage, arrive at a marriage equal to
that of Mistress Anne Russell, put to silence all
discussion about the past, and regain security for
her future. That under such circumstances she
was taken advantage of by a man of exceptional
rapacity in this respect, who then refused her, and
covered her with obloquy, not only crushed her
hopes and excited a general comment, but in all
probability reacted heavily upon the poet-actor,
Shakspeare himself, among those who knew the
circumstances, if, that is, he had in fact been earlier
attracted by her, and had been therefore also
involved, an issue which depends upon the principal thesis of this Note, whether Mary Fytton
was, or was not, the "Dark Lady" of the sonnets,
and also upon the further question of the date and
interpretation of Sonnets CXVI-CXXVI addressed
to Lord Southampton.

The delicate and exquisite lyric, CXLV, was
probably among the first addressed to the "Dark
Lady" by Shakspeare, and remains as a witness
to their first relation.

> Those lips that Love's own hand did make
> Breathed forth the sound that said "I hate,"
> To me that languished for her sake:

But when she saw my woeful state,
Straight in her heart did mercy come,
Chiding that tongue that ever sweet,
Was used in giving gentle doom;
And taught it thus anew to greet;
"I hate" she altered with an end,
That followed it as gentle day
Doth follow night, who like a fiend
From heaven to hell is flown away.
   "I hate" from hate away she threw,
   And saved my life, saying "not you."

The exultant and lover-like lines seem to have been written almost extempore.

The *Sidney Papers* give a faint and conjectural light upon some incidents immediately preceding the Russell wedding, which might have occurred so had Mary Fytton been the "Dark Lady" of the sonnets; on the other hand, they are susceptible of other explanations. The letters were written to Lord Herbert's uncle, who seems to have been continually interested in Mistress Fytton. The dates of the letters are altered to the present usage:

My Lord Harbert taking Yesternight his Leave of Lord Nottingham and Sir R. Cecil . . . Lord Harbert is highly favored by the Queen, for at his Departure, he had Access unto her, and was private an Howre; but he greatly wants Advise, and extremely longes for you here.

Baynard's Castell, Nov. 29, 1599.

Her Majestie is in very good Health, and comes much abroad these Holidayes, for almost every Night she is in the Presence, to see the Ladies dawnce the old and new country Dawnces, with the Taber and Pipe. . . . My Lord Harbert is sicke of his Tertian Ague at Ramesbury.

Richmond, this Twelve Eve, Jan. 5, 1600.

Mrs. Fitton is sicke, and gon from Court to her Father's. Mrs. Onslow doth Exceed the rest in Bravery, which is noted. Mrs. Southwell is now one of the Nomber. [These were Maids of Honour.]

Baynard's Castell, Jan. 12, 1600.

My Lord Harbert, . . . is fallen to have his Ague again, and no Hope of his being here, before Easter, which I am sorry for.

Baynard's Castell, Jan. 24, 1600.

Lady Sidney, wife of Sir Robert Sidney, the uncle of Lord Herbert, "visited Mrs. Fitton, that hath long bene here sicke in London."

Baynard's Castell, Feb. 21, 1600.

My Lord Harbert came on Wednesday night, and within this Howre he goes to the Court; I find him exceedingly desirous to see you.

Baynard's Castell, March 15, 1600.

Mr. Whyte seems, in the first letter of November 29, 1599, and perhaps again in the last, of March 15, 1600, to have felt some anxiety about Lord

Herbert, and this may have been aroused by Lord Herbert's conduct in respect to Mary Fytton, as that, soon after March, 1600, led to the later and absolute displeasure of the Queen. Lord Herbert, at the time when Mr. Whyte wrote the earlier letter, that of November 29, 1599, had left the Court. Mary Fytton, also, appears to have left the Court, and to have gone to, or, perhaps taken refuge with, her father, on a plea of sickness, some time before January 12, 1600, a month later than Lord Herbert's departure. This was not at her father's house at Gawsworth but at his house in London—that her father had a house in London is established by a letter dated from it, and appearing in Lady Newdegate's Fytton Letters—where her father may have been. At all events, the young lady was in London when Lady Sidney, who was Lord Herbert's aunt by marriage, called on her toward the end of February, 1600, and she had been there, and not at Court, for what Mr. Whyte calls a "long" period, certainly from early in January. Lord Herbert was away from Court, at Ramsbury, Newbury, and Wilton, from November 29, 1599, to mid-March, 1600, when he returned. Mary was thinking of returning to Court, as appears to be very probable from the last letter quoted further on from Sir William Knollys' correspondence, some time after the above letter of February 21, 1600, and not far from the time of Lord Herbert's return to the Court in March, her return to health nearly coinciding with his return to Court. These weeks or months of her absence were not long before her fatal error, and about a year after the time—basing this time upon the first arrival of Lord Herbert at the Court in the latter part of June, 1598, and the probable progress of the "Dark Lady" sonnets—when, according to the Fytton theory of the sonnets, the influence of the actor-dramatist upon her had been repelled by her in favour of Lord Herbert. Considering the incident, there seems to have been some cause for her prolonged absence from Court, and it appears hardly to be accounted for by illness in a prominent girl of twenty-one, and who was to be the leader of the marriage dance of June 16th, a scene in which she appeared to advantage, an enviable distinction, due doubtless to her own attraction and ability, but rather to have depended upon Lord Herbert's absence. It seems that during this time of absence she was able to receive Sir William Knollys. If the story of the sonnets of 1599, two of the most inculpating in the "Dark Lady" series, should be taken as referring to her, it is an evident inference that she may have feared to remain

longer at Court in Lord Herbert's absence, that
is, that she could not trust herself to remain there.
Her absence from Court when Lord Herbert was
absent accords precisely with the theory that she
was the "Dark Lady." And there we must leave
it. In accordance with the theory, it may be said
of her departure from Court during Lord Herbert's
departure that, while there may have been various
reasons for it, still, if this too adventurous young
lady had conceived a true passion for the already
married playwright, had become very gravely
entangled in it, and feared the world's judgment
upon it, such might her conduct have been. Questionable as the point is, and valuable only as cor-
roborative evidence, it is certainly true that her
actions correspond to what might be expected, if her
interest in the poet was such as has been supposed.

The reader may care to see that the conduct of
Lord Herbert, who has a certain place in the history of the sonnets, was not unobserved by those
who were watching him. Whyte writes to Herbert's uncle, two months after the Russell wedding:

My Lord Harbert is very well. I now heare litle
of that Matter intended by the Earl of Nottingham,
[Admiral Lord Charles Howard of Effingham, chief
in command of the English fleet against the Spanish

Armada], towards hym; only I observe he makes very much of hym; but I don't find any Disposicion at all in this gallant young Lord to marry.

London, Aug. 16, 1600.

The intentions of the Earl of Nottingham toward Lord Herbert seem to have been in the direction of a matrimonial arrangement, but which did not take place. Two months later Mr. Whyte also writes:

My Lord Harbert wilbe all the next Weeke at Greenwich, to practise at Tilt. He often wishes you here. Beleve me, my Lord, he is a very gallant Gentleman, and indeed wants such a Frend as you are neare unto him.

Penshurst, Oct. 18, 1600.

Mr. Whyte's uneasiness was soon shown to have adequate cause.

A letter of reminiscence in the Public Record Office, and written a year or more after the event, records how Mary Fytton used to throw a cloak about her, and depart from the Court to meet Lord Herbert:

In that time when that Mrs. Fytton was in great favour, and one of her Majesty's Maids of Honour, and during the time that the Earl of Pembroke favoured her, she would put off her head-tire, and tuck up her clothes, and take a large, white cloak, and march as though she had been a man to meet the said Earl out of the Court.

S. P., Dom. Add., vol. xxxiv.

Initiative and resolution, and also freedom of movement, would not have been wanting to her, if she had been attracted toward the great dramatist. Soon after leaving the Court, she seems to have gone to her ever constant sister, Anne, at Arbury; her misfortune was condoned by her family, and she was recognized by some at least of her friends. Subsequently, in 1606, she was in grave fault again, ascribed, most probably, to a Captain William Polwhele, whom she then married. The story, doubtless exaggerated, credits her with two or even three illegitimate children. Her mother, Lady Fytton, whose husband, Sir Edward, had lately died, writes in 1606 to Anne, then become Lady Newdigate, at Arbury:

I take no joye to heer of your sister nor of that boy. If it hade plesed God when I did bear her that shee and I hade bine beried, it hade saved mee ffrom a great delle of sorow and gryffe, and her ffrom sham and such shame as never hade Chesshyre woman, worse now than ever. Wrytt no mor to mee of her.

Gossip from a Muniment Room, 1st Ed., p. 76.

A postscript follows which is less stern. Later, Lady Fytton, writing again, probably in 1607, to her daughter, Anne, Lady Newdigate, says:

My ladi ffrancis [Frances] saed she [Mary] was the vyles woman under the sone [sun]. . . . But

Poullwhyll is a very kave [knave?], and taketh the disgrace of his wyff and all her ffryndes to make the wordt
[world?] thynk hym worthey of her, and that she des-
sarved no bettar. It is longe to wrytt all I knowe.
. . . Thus praying God to defend us ffrom our
enymes and blese us, I end, remaynyng ever your
poure, kynde, greved mother,

A. FFYTON.

Gossip from a Muniment Room, 1st Ed., p. 79.

Mary Polwhele, becoming herself a widow, is
afterwards mentioned in the Fytton Letters, in
1611 or 1612, as probably with Anne, her sister,
then also a widow, at Arbury, and the record of the
Fytton Letters makes it certain that Mary, whatever her demerits, was still of such merit as to be
recognized by her sister. Still later, Mary married
John Lougher, whom also she survived, dying
finally in 1647, after surviving all, apparently, with
whom she had been connected in her earlier years,
her parents, brothers and sister, and amid the fall
of the Monarchy and Court in which she had lived.

In reading these sonnets and estimating the possibility that a man in Shakspeare's position, an
humble actor and mere playwright, might form an
attachment for a lady of high place at the Court,
we must not forget that he was, though obscured
by circumstance, the unapproached King of English literature, and that he had in him the power

and grace which made him famous, after his day, for his then little appreciated merits, his high point of view and his wide comprehension of the world in which he lived, his passion for truth, his wit, and his sense of form which kept even his prolific pen in check, his insight into human nature and his power of describing its most secret recesses, his wide tolerance, his range from the poetic to a scientific estimate of life—the catalogue of his merits is a long one, and, besides this, the testimony of those who knew him, as to his disposition, is distinctly to his credit. He was a man thirty-three years old in 1597, and recognized by the nobility, and by the Court and perhaps by the Queen, not certainly but probably, in that year, through his Sir John Falstaff. It would not then be either impossible or unprecedented that an undisciplined but intelligent young lady of the Court, as was Mary Fytton, should come to entertain for him a more than passing regard.

An analysis of his relation to Lord Southampton, the probable dedicatee of the majority of the sonnets, indicates, when the sonnets are carefully studied, that this relation was, to a certain extent, that which was due to his character, mental ascendency and literary achievements, though conventionally lowered by his actor's profession, and that he was by no means the mere client of that nobleman which seems sometimes to be assumed. The fact is far otherwise, his private relations with Lord Southampton having been on a basis of natural equality and genuine friendship. (Sonnets CXX, CXXV, L, LXXI, LXXII, etc.) That he advanced from such a situation of favour (Sonnet CXII, 12), so far as to permit himself to be drawn into relations with a lady of the Court is not, when the statement is viewed from this standpoint, essentially improbable, nor will such a history be put aside as impossible.

From an examination of her life, it appears that Mary Fytton, although distinguished at Court, admired and attractive, still was one among the enigmas of womankind, ladies dangerous to themselves and others, and this gives additional strength to the theory that it was she to whom, notwithstanding her high station, Shakspeare became attached, and who is so curiously, that is, condemningly and admiringly, described in the sonnets. As to her second fault in 1606, it is on record that her husband, Polwhele, was recognized in 1608, two years later, by her great-uncle, Francis Fytton, in his Will, who left to him "my usual riding sword, being damasked, commonly called a fauchion, and my best horse or gelding of mine, to his own best

liking, as a remembrance and token of my love to him
and to his now wife," and that her sister, Lady Newdigate, remained kind to her.   There may, therefore, have been considerations which lessened the
judgment which we are now inclined to pass upon
her, and also, probably, great personal attraction.

Shakspeare's part in this long-past tragedy, now
more than three centuries old, was, as we read the
sonnets, the subject of his humiliated but still
noble answer, in a sonnet written, most probably,
circa 1599, to Lord Southampton, and it is a part
of the record of the dramatist's difference with and
formal withdrawal as a client from him (Sonnets
CXVI-CXXVI):

'Tis better to be vile than vile esteemed,
When not to be receives reproach of being;
And the just pleasure lost, which is so deemed
Not by our feeling, but by others' seeing.
For why should others' false adulterate eyes
Give salutation to my sportive blood?
Or on my frailties why are frailer spies,
Which in their wills count bad what I think good?
No, I am that I am, and they that level
At my abuses reckon up their own;
I may be straight though they themselves be bevel;
By their rank thoughts my deeds must not be shown,
   Unless this general evil they maintain,
   All men are bad and in their badness reign.

Sonnet CXXI.

A similar expression to that in line 9, "I am that I am," may be found in I Corinthians, xv, 10, and see in *Othello*, Iago's words, I, i, 65.

THE RESULT TO SHAKSPEARE

The subject of this Note, an inquiry mainly as to who was the lady to whom the sonnets to the "Dark Lady" were written, is certainly an ungrateful one, and it might seem, at first thought, to make little difference whether Shakspeare's irregularity and his unhappiness were concerned with Mary Fytton or another, but the question perhaps goes beyond a mere question of names; this episode in his life, as Mary Fytton was a young lady highly connected and prominent at the Court, if this theory of the love-affair is accepted, possibly affected unfavourably his relations with his friend, the Earl of Southampton, who had been abroad during much of the year 1598, the year in which most of the "Dark Lady" sonnets were written, and who also had just married, as well as those with the Earl of Pembroke, and accordingly his

standing with the nobility in general, while so
great a check upon his social advancement, especially with Lord Southampton (Sonnets CXIX,
CXX, CXXI, CXXV), may have made a profound
change in the course of his life, and affected his
later plays. There must be some method for un-
ravelling the incidents of the time, and the following representation of them has seemed to us to
perhaps accord with the conditions in Shakspeare's
life, as we understand it, and to give a slight clue
also to the motives perceptible in some of his later
work. During eight months of the year 1598 Lord
Southampton was abroad in France (he embarked
at Dover for Dieppe with Sir Robert Cecil's Em-
bassy to France, Feb. 17, and protracted his stay
in France, after the return of Sir Robert, until
after October 16), excepting his brief and hasty
trip back to England to marry, under circumstances which made marriage necessary for the
lady, and which had been much commented upon;
when Lord Southampton finally returned to England, where he was immediately arrested and for a
short time imprisoned by the Queen, for his marriage with a Maid of Honour without the Queen's
previous consent, he, and even more Lady Southampton, would assuredly be scrupulously careful
as to their own standing in every kind of circum-

stance, and especially as to the character of their slightest acquaintance, the Queen retaining her displeasure. Lady Southampton would be even more careful than her husband as to their acquaintance, whether people of their own rank, or clients, or of indeterminate standing such as that of Shakspeare with Lord Southampton, she seeming to have felt even more than he the weight of the Queen's anger. A letter of John Chamberlain's to Dudley Carleton is to the effect that "the newcoined Countess" was dismissed with much contumely from her place at Court, and committed to "the best-appointed lodging in the Fleet" prison, as the Queen's answer to her conduct. (*Dict. of Nat. Biography, Art.*, Henry Wriothesley.) Lady Southampton's influence over her husband was, no doubt greater than that of Shakspeare. The poet's apparent presumption in respect to a Maid of Honour during Lord Southampton's absence from England might result, first, in Lord Southampton's attitude of reserve towards him, and then in the breach of their friendship, both of which seem to be recorded, or distinctly referred to, in sonnets which were almost certainly written at this time. Shakspeare's original acquaintance with the Maid of Honour—Lord Herbert, as we remember, came to the Court about June, 1598—would not have

been considered important by Lord Southampton,
if he noticed it at all, who, then unmarried, and
having returned from the Azores Expedition not
far from the beginning of the last week in October,
in '1597' left England early in 1598. The poet
appears to have declined to accept anything less
from Lord Southampton than a true friendship.
He writes:

No, let me be obsequious in thy heart,
And take thou my oblation, poor but free,
Which is not mixed with seconds, knows no art,
But mutual render, only me for thee.
    Hence, thou suborned informer! a true soul ·
    When most impeached stands least in thy control.
Sonnet CXXV.

After the public disgrace and dismissal of Mistress Fytton, which occurred a little over a year
later, probably, and which was not alleviated by
marriage, the consequences to the actor-poet with
Lord and Lady Southampton, and also among his
more valued friends at Court, would certainly be
most serious if he was known to have been involved
and if such consequences occurred, they could not
fail to be reflected in his work. We approach with
some diffidence a reading of these plays from this
point of view, as they have been the subjects of so
many varying impressions of them, not including

this, but we still submit some tentative suggestions
as to several of them, upon the foundation of an
assumed acceptance of the Shakspeare-Herbert-
Fytton hypothesis. The first shadow, which syn-
chronizes closely with the known course of events
in the lives of Lord Southampton and Lord
Herbert, appears in *As You Like It* (1599), but
evidence of a distinct change in the poet's disposition, and of a change not lightly to be accounted
for, is found in *All's Well That Ends Well* and
Measure for Measure, the second written, the first,
it is understood, rewritten, with a new title, within
the years immediately succeeding the exposure in
1601 of the Herbert-Fytton scandal; the first seems
to go so far as to allude almost openly to Lord
Southampton, and it reflects also, with a degree of
condemnation very unusual in representations in
the theatre, upon the failing then publicly attached
to the name of the Earl of Pembroke, the one
nobleman being at the time confined in the Tower
of London, and the other debarred from Court.
The two plays, as will be at once admitted, are
unlike their predecessors in a grave and critical,
at times censorious tone, employed upon most
caustic elements of story; coming together, when
Shakspeare was in the full tide of his power, they
present a question which seems to call for an an-

swer. We notice in the former play, in a scene especially constructed for it, doubtless in the revision, the appointment of Bertram as General of the Horse (III, iii, 1), which had been Lord Southampton's position in Ireland until he was removed from it; he was appointed "Lord General of the Horse in Ireland" by warrant dated April 15, 1599, and was removed from the position in the following summer, on the Queen's reiterated command much to his and Essex's discomfiture. In mentioning this, Shakspeare alluded to a point on which Southampton must necessarily have been sensitive. We find another coincidence in the reference to the size of the army in Italy in the play, which, doubtfully said to be twenty or twenty-one thousand men, is that of Essex's army in Ireland, with which Southampton served, excepting an increase in the proportion of Horse. (IV, iii, 151, 190.) Camden says of the army in Ireland in 1599: "His army was allotted him [Essex], as much as he would desire, neither ever saw Ireland a greater, 16,000 foot, 1300 Horse, which number afterwards in all was compleat 20,000." (*Annales, trans. Browne,* vol. 2, p. 239.) We notice in Bertram's self-will and childishness a parallel with Southampton's character, which, as is well established, was similar, and in both respects. It is clear that the play contained in its earliest draught Bertram's *status* as a royal ward, as that is an essential part in the original Italian story; it is equally clear therefore that the poet must have chosen at the time of revising the draught, in 1602 probably, to take up a draught containing a structural and considerable likeness to the career of Southampton, he having been conspicuously a royal ward from his early boyhood. This resemblance, when it is read in the light of the other resemblances in the play already noted, is considerable evidence that Shakspeare had Southampton in mind when undertaking the revision of the play. The incident of the wardship is taken from the story of Beltramo and Giletta in *The Palace of Pleasure*, from which the play was devised. Lord Herbert, also, was for less than three months a royal ward. (Pembroke's letter of June 19, 1601, *supra.*) The probable and usually admitted change in the title of the play, from *Love's Labour's Won* to *All's Well that Ends Well*, is a change in the direction of this understanding of the circumstances under which the play was rewritten. There is also found in the play a description of unbridled license, which, if it were a citation of the Earl of Pembroke for his recent and then notorious fault, would read much alike. (IV, ii; IV, iii, 17–35, 248, 333; Sonnet XL, 13; XCV, 6.)

Bertram, in whom these incidents are united, is a strikingly unworthy character; if the poet had been so far humiliated as to show his resentment against Southampton for his injustice and desertion—and to Lord Southampton the final sonnets of separation were, beyond a just doubt, addressed—and his censure of the viciousness of Pembroke, he could have seen in this play as complete an expression of those sentiments as the circumstances allowed.

The second play, *Measure for Measure* (1603), contains a personal allusion, probably, while an estimate of this play is much aided by keeping the author's sense of injustice done to him, and its probable cause, in the reader's mind. We notice, for instance, the Duke as a detective in his city, the bitter description of civic corruption (III, ii, 240; V, i, 318), the sexual statute enforced against Claudio, the downfall of Angelo through Claudio's sister, the insistence on the "seeming" deception of society (I, iii, 54; II, iv, 149; III, ii, 40, 41; *cf. Hamlet*, I, ii, 76, 83), some lines which may be thought, perhaps, to have a personal accent (I, ii, 120–127; I, iv, 80–83; III, i, 5), the song to Mariana and the Duke's admonition as to her music (IV, i, 1, 14; Sonnet CXXVIII; *A. and Cleo.*, II, v, 1), the peculiar allusion to "the moated grange" as the "dejected" Mariana's residence, suggested possibly by Mary's residence in exile (III, i, 277)—Mariana, we observe, is an addition by the poet to the older literature of this story, and the similarity of the name to Mary's is worth notice—and, finally, the disregard of rank in the Duke's marriage to Isabella; the incidents of the play might be the poetic reflex of a reverse in Shakspeare's life in 1601, and the tone of settled disillusionment seems to have been retained, unbroken, though with ultimate modification, through the remaining part, the more serious and grander part, of his dramatic career.

In *All's Well that Ends Well* (III, v), among the neighbours of Diana are Mariana and the speechless Violenta, the latter name taken from William Painter's *Palace of Pleasure*, but the former appears again to be the poet's selection.

Mr. William Smith in his *History of Warwickshire* (1829), mentions a circumstance which is of not a little interest in relation to Mary's possible residence after leaving the Court. He says (p. 150), "At a short distance from Harbury [Arbury] Park is a farm called Temple house. The building was formerly surrounded by a moat, and in the front are still the remains of a lofty painted [pointed] window, which is the only principal relic

of this ancient building." It is conceivable that
Mary was lodged here, near her sister, the mistress
of Arbury, after returning for a time to Gawsworth,
her father's house in Cheshire, as it seems that she
did, and this would correspond remarkably with
"the moated grange" in *Measure for Measure*.
It appears that Mary went to Arbury in no great
length of time after leaving the Court; she was
there in January, 1603 (*Fytton Letters*, 1st ed.,
pp. 42, 52, 55, 71, 72). The family at Arbury then
consisted of Mr. and Mrs. Newdigate and their
three young children, the eldest a daughter named
after Mary, and amusingly called "little wasps-
nest," and nearly five years old. Mr. Newdigate
might at first prefer to keep a certain distance between Mrs. Newdigate and the children and their
aunt. A little further evidence in support of this
definition of the "moated grange" can be also
found. Small, moated enclosures, of an unpreten-
tious type, were at the time numerous in England,
and the term was familiar to Shakspeare, whose
early life was spent in Warwickshire. In a paper
on *The Antiquities of Warwickshire* (1875), Mr. M.
H. Bloxham says (p. 9):

Ancient British and Roman fortifications must not
be confounded with those numerous moated areas
scattered all over the kingdom, of which perhaps there

are not less than 100 in this county, the moats of which
when filled with water, inclose an area of from a rood
to two acres in extent, and these, to which no precise
history is attached, I take to have been formed for
mere defensive operations in the reigns of Stephen,
John and Henry III in the intestine wars which then
prevailed.

Shakspeare, therefore, probably knew these con-
structions. A notice of Temple House, whose moat
was perhaps constructed by the Knights Templars,
but which has long been an adjacent and doubtless
subsidiary building to Arbury Hall and the preceding Priory, will be found in Kelly's *Directory
of Warwickshire* (1888), where it is mentioned that
(46):

Temple House, in this parish, is supposed to have
formerly belonged to the Knights Templars; it is now
a farm house. . . .   The manor in the 28th of Elizabeth (1586), passed . . . to John Newdegate. . . .
Arbury Hall still remains in possession of the Newdegate family.

In 1601, when Mary left the Court, her sister had
been in residence as mistress of Arbury about six
years. On the Ordnance Map of England, Temple
House is conspicuously designated, and is but a
half mile from Arbury Hall, which stands in an
enclosed Park of perhaps 300 acres. Sir William
Dugdale, in *The Antiquities of Warwickshire*

(1656), uses the word "grange" of landed property in this vicinity, and it is generally so used, and mentions a grant to the Knights Templars within the parish, Chilvers Coton, in which Temple House is situated, in the reign of Henry II (p. 770); it is interesting to note that he also traces the title of the Newdigate family to Arbury from the heirs of a Duke of Suffolk and the dissolution of the monasteries in Henry VIII's time. The monastery at Arbury, Erdburie Priory, which immediately preceded the dwelling, Arbury Hall, acquired by the Newdigates, presumably held the use of the nearby building of the Knights Templars. Aubrey, in the Seventeenth century, speaks of a similar use of a farm house by a monastery, saying: "The Manor House, (which was, I think, a grange to the Abbey of Malmesbury)," and says also, interestingly for Americans, that it "was for the greatest part re-edified by Sir Lawrance Washington about the beginning of the Civil Wars" (Aubrey's *Wiltshire*, Part I). The Order of Knights Templars was discontinued in England *circa* 1308, in the reign of Edward II, and their building at Temple House had therefore been turned to other uses, chiefly of the monastery, for nearly three centuries at the time when Mary's residence was determined by her family. It seems very reasonable to suppose that the term "moated grange" refers to an enclosure and building similar to that at Temple House, as it was probably used in Mary's time, and, if that is admitted, Shakspeare's reference to such a grange as the residence of the "dejected Mariana" is in language which corresponds with this peculiar establishment of farm building near Arbury Hall. The phrase hardly applies to the lady in the play, who was living in a city. It seems clear that the poet went so far as to ascribe to Mariana a residence which is inappropriate to the circumstances of the play. On the face of the evidence, the inference is probable that the poet had some thought foreign to the play in his mind when he wrote, "there at the moated grange resides this dejected Mariana."

Measure for Measure, then, contains elements which show that Shakspeare had changed in disposition, and a phrase in the play suggests also that he may have had in mind the exile of Mary Fytton.

We may consider this influence upon Shakspeare's later plays a little further. The two plays just commented upon are but slighter works, written while producing a much greater, *Hamlet* (1602-3-4), in which his troubled mind is represented in ghostly imagery. An analysis of the play from this standpoint leads to little which can be verified but can easily be carried on by the reader, who will find that it brings to him many suggestions upon the text, suggestions which will vary probably with each reader who attempts to define them. The personal accent is remarkable, and perhaps gives to the play much of its attraction. From our standpoint, Hamlet's attitude is one of irresolution when under great provocation.

The childish sedition of Essex, with the execution of Essex, whom the poet had supported with a loving tribute during the campaign in Ireland, and the arrest of Southampton early in 1601, and the death of Shakspeare's father in that year, as well as the tragedy of Mary Fytton, had each a part in making this a year of change. Some lines, written for *Hamlet* but afterwards cancelled, well express the dramatist's altered spirit:

O Time, how swiftly runs our joys away!
 Content on Earth was never certain bred;
 Today we laugh and live, tomorrow dead.
Q. 1, Sc. XIII, 42.

Such depression differs from anything we see in *Troilus and Cressida* or *Twelfth Night* or *Julius Cæsar* or their predecessors. The poet's mind and manner changed with the century. The accuracy of the text is dubious, but the sentiment of the lines is probably authentic. The same too pessimistic sentiment of the last line is again perceptible in *Measure for Measure* (III, i, 5), and in *Hamlet* (I, ii, 129), and elsewhere in the two plays. An allusion in *Hamlet* to the critical year, 1601, occurs, perhaps, in the scene in the churchyard:

> By the Lord, Horatio, this three years I have taken note of it; the age is grown so picked that the toe of the peasant comes so near the heel of the courtier, he galls his kibe.
>
> *Q. 2 and Folio, V, i, 150.*

If this reflection is dated in 1604, the date of the second Quarto, its unnecessary but definite specification of time dates back to the year of the exposure of the scandal, 1601. The poet says that for three years he had had occasion to notice that the age was so critical that the lower pressed on the higher orders, a limitation of time which is comprehensible if we think that during those three years the poet had been censured for precisely that disregard of rank, or for presumption. In the preceding Quarto, the first Quarto, the phrase is: "This seven years I have noted it," the specification of seven years being perhaps meant for any indefinite period of time, or the poet perhaps not caring then to be more precise, but it is made de-

finite in the second Quarto. It is difficult to rely
on the first Quarto, but the second is of primary
authority. In the following incident in this scene,
it is certainly a fact that the time allotted by the
grave-digger for the jester, Yorick's interment,
23 years, is the age, or nearly the age, of Mary
Fytton in 1601, when she was sent from the Court.
This period appears in the first Quarto as "this
dozen year," and in this instance also a period
indefinite in the first Quarto is made definite and
particular in the second. There can be no reliance
on the first Quarto in such a matter of numerals,
but the text of the second Quarto is fundamental;
Shakspeare seldom if ever uses words without
meaning. The number of years might be an allusion to the day of his birth, the 23rd of April, if
the 23rd is the exact date, or to something else,
but if we take into consideration the immediately
preceding seeming allusion to 1601, and possibly to
Mary Fytton's history in that year, the inference
is not without reason, and the point has a corrob-
orative value, very doubtful as the evidence is.

To carry the theory a step further. Subject to
the exigencies of the stage and to his dramatic
genius, Iago, in the next play (1604), might be a
figure of his self-accusation as to, and implication
in, the intrigue and its result, Othello of his heart-

break. It was, perhaps, as in *Hamlet*, his deep, personal interest in events which he had in mind, which gives to the play its life-likeness and absorbing interest. Macbeth, in his final and darker moments, in the following play (1605), might represent his cancelled ambition, and the emptiness of worldly glory; by these suggestions and references be it understood merely, that the springs of some of the words and delineations of these characters could be attributed to his connection with the unhappy fate of Mary Fytton. This is carrying the theory a great way, but if the ascription of his sonnets to Mary Fytton is once admitted, the rest follows, as we are inclined to think, almost inevitably. A resemblance of the "Dark Lady" to "Cleopatra" (1607–8), has been ventured by Professor Dowden.

There may be a reminiscence of the lady of the sonnets in the following passage:

Whose beauty did astonish the survey
Of richest eyes, whose words all ears took captive,
Whose dear perfection hearts that scorned to serve
Humbly called mistress.
All's Well that Ends Well, V, *iii*, *16*.

The last two impassioned lines go somewhat past the necessities of the play; in truth, the two lines, or rather line and a half, have nothing to do with Helena's precisely contrary experience. The poet's foredoomed love-affair with Mary Fytton, if it existed, cannot but arouse the sympathy of everyone who is cognizant of the strength of the affection, and can estimate the corresponding pain which must have attended its hapless result.

The past few pages perhaps illustrate the customary weakness of reading one's own views into the works of the great dramatist, but the references will at least suggest how considerable might be the result in Shakspearean interpretation, if the hypothesis as to Mary Fytton were accepted.

The interpretation of Sonnets CXVI–CXXVI and some others, the ascription of those sonnets to Lord Southampton, and their connection with the question of Shakspeare's passion for Mary Fytton, are subjects so intertwined and extensive that they cannot be taken up here; their interpretation necessarily involves the question of the relation of Shakspeare to Lord Southampton, and therefore of the sonnets as a whole which he addressed to that nobleman.

The result to Shakspeare, if this view is admitted, seems to have been to isolate him within himself, that is, to debar him from familiar association with the friends whom he most enjoyed, and from all such openings for his ambition as,

through them, the strife for position at the Court
might present.   This later attitude of his, sometimes called that of a detached critic of the world
he lived in, has been often observed.   In his earlier
plays this is not so.   In *Love's Labour's Lost* he
was, none more so, frankly a part of the Elizabethan world about him, and no substantial loss
of his first, fresh enthusiasm can be observed until
after *Much Ado about Nothing* (1598–9).   His life
doubtless was always single and individual, but it
became with all the strength and armour of the
mind, peculiar to himself.   Perhaps in *Measure for
Measure* his detachment first receives a definite
expression; some lines in the scene between the
Duke and the Friar (I, iii, 1), might be taken as
the representative portrayal of his change of spirit,
as well as of garment.   *Twelfth Night*, somewhat
earlier (1599–1600), the last of his Comedies,
received his finest finish.

To sum up, in their main outline, the facts of
this abstract, as far as we have gone, and our in-
ferences from them, we have, at the commencement of the story, Rosaline, seeming perhaps as a
representation drawn from life (1597), a sonnet
taken from her description and written to a lady
resembling her in dark complexion and character,
and Mary Fytton then at Court, then others of

Shakspeare's "Dark Lady" sonnets, written perhaps before 1599, those indicating some one, "my sweetest friend," supplanting the poet in his affection, then, probably in 1599, the sonnets describing the writer as thus distressed,

> Past cure I am, now reason is past care,
> And frantic-mad with evermore unrest.
>   *Sonnet CXLVII.*

pleading with the lady, indicating also rejection, severance and self-questioning, then the sonnets, separate in the Quarto, to a young and successful rival, and, at the end of the story, Lord Herbert and Mary Fytton, all in about three years, from mid 1597, when the revision of *Love's Labour's Lost*, and also the sonnet taken from it, were written, to mid 1600, when Mary Fytton made her great misstep.

THE ARBURY PORTRAITS

A view that Mary Fytton was fair of complexion, which would overthrow the theory that she was the "Dark Lady" of the sonnets, has been founded upon a double portrait, on panel, of two ladies at Arbury, in Warwickshire, and an account of the picture has been given in Lady Newdegate's *Gossip from a Muniment Room*, the Fytton Letters. Although the editor of the Letters, and owner or possessor of the portrait, has the advantage of an acquaintance with it, some suggestions may still be advanced upon the reproductions of that, and of a second portrait, on canvas, which accompany the book. (*Frontispiece and at p. 76.*)

The portraits are said to be of the sisters, Anne and Mary Fytton, the double portrait being of both the sisters and the second portrait of Mary alone. While Lady Newdegate states her view as to the faces and expressions of the two ladies, though her opinion, as she very candidly admits, is not wholly free from doubt, Mr. C. G. O. Bridgeman, who adds an Appendix to the book, depends mainly upon the inscription on the double portrait, proving its accuracy by the known dates of birth of the Fytton sisters, the inscription, he tells us, stating the age of each of the ladies accurately, at the time of painting the portrait. This accuracy does not meet the main issue, for if the inscription were a subsequent addition to the portrait, and we think that this is clearly demonstrable, it would follow the Parish register, or other record, and an

The Statues of Anne (*Left*) and Mary Fytton (*Right*)
in the Church of St. James, at Gawsworth

agreement with the records could prove nothing
but its own correctness in that respect, and not the
time when it was placed upon the portrait. The
identification with the two Fytton sisters is not
supported by any likeness to each other of the
ladies in the portraits, and it becomes wholly
untenable, as to Mary, when the portraits are men-
tally placed beside the faces and figures of the un-
doubted statues of the two sisters in the church
at Gawsworth, while the two other elements of
internal evidence in the double portrait, the inscription and the Fytton pansy, on which the identification is based, prove, on examination, to be very
hazy witnesses. As to the cardinal question, the
appearance of the two ladies in the double portrait,
we cannot see in the faces themselves any reason
whatsoever for holding that the lady on the right,
the alleged Mary Fytton, is the younger of the
two, nor that she is the sister of the lady on the
left; she seems to us to be decidedly the elder, and
there is, to us, no family resemblance at all between them. If the face of the so-called Mary
Fytton is the face of a girl of fourteen years and a
fraction, we have never seen another like instance,
nor do we think it is credible that a girl of those
years would be so maturely represented. She appears to us, if not of quite as old a face as that

given later in Lady Newdegate's book as that of
the high-bred and dignified young lady in the magnificent Court dress, in the second portrait, still
nearer to it than to the earlier age. The absence
of any family resemblance between the two ladies
is confirmed more strikingly if, after comparing
the lady on the right with the lady on the left, in
the double portrait, we bring into the comparison
also the lady in Court dress, in whom this difference is accentuated. We can say deliberately
that there is not a lineament or expression in these
portraits which tends to show a relation other than
that of mere friendship between the ladies, and
that nothing suggests, in the likeness of the lady
on the right in the double portrait, in face, bearing,
jewels or dress, the early age of fourteen years.

As to the symbolic evidence of the flowers and
leaves which are given to the two ladies by the
artist, it is said that two of the flowers are distinguishable as pansies in the double portrait;
in the photogravure they are not perfectly deter-
minable. The pansy was an heraldic device of the
Fyttons. If the conspicuous leaf painted on the
right sleeve of the lady on the right, called Mary
Fytton, is that of an holly, as Mr. Bridgeman in
his careful description says it is, it modifies the
signification of the pansy held by the lady as one

among her other flowers. As Mr. Bridgeman is
silent as to the holly, beyond merely mentioning
it, no claim is made for the Fyttons of the holly as
an emblem. There is also a spray, described as
resembling a palm, on her left sleeve. That also
is not said by Mr. Bridgeman to have any significance in respect to the Fyttons, and if the holly
and the palm are considered to have a significance,
as they certainly have, they seem to denote the
lady as of a different family. The pansy has an
heraldic intention, but its significance attached
only to the admitted daughter of the Fyttons
Anne, on the left, on whose ruff a pansy is painted,
not at all to the other lady on the right, who merely
holds a pansy as a single part of her bouquet, and
probably as a compliment to a friend and honoured guest at Gawsworth. There is further
evidence, and it is perhaps decisive, from these
flowers. Mr. Bridgeman says of the lady on the
left: "On her ruff is painted a pansy." Mr. Tyler,
who has seen the original portrait at Arbury, says
that the lady on the right, the so-called Mary
Fytton, has a "carnation or clove" on her ruff.
Mr. Bridgeman says of her: "On her ruff is depicted a carnation." Why not a pansy, if the
flowers are thus painted as heraldic devices, and
the two ladies are sisters? The deduction from the

leaves and flowers is contrary to the theory that the lady on the right represents the younger sister, and is in favour of the view that the representation is of some friend of the family, in whose bouquet a pansy was placed, and this accords with the conclusion derived from the faces of the ladies as to their mutual relation.

To go a step further in estimating this floral evidence, both the ladies hold in their left hands flowers, the lady on the right her bouquet, and Anne holding a carnation, which is possibly linked by this floral symbolism with the carnation painted on the ruff of her companion, thus denoting again the friendly bond between them. There is an evident balance in the floral decoration, Anne having the Fytton pansy on her ruff, which flower the other lady holds in the bouquet in her left hand, that lady having a carnation on her ruff, which flower again Anne holds in her left hand. This seems rather the symbolism of friendship and not that of sisters. Mr. Bridgeman has apparently anticipated this point, for he seems to claim (p. 168), that the carnation was also a family flower of the Fyttons, but the evidence which he brings forward for it is curiously weak, that which he cites consisting of the recurrence of a carnation in another family portrait of Anne, taken as Lady

Newdigate, long after, with an infant at Arbury; the recurrence of the carnation proves nothing of Mr. Bridgeman's contention, but only that her preference for carnations still existed, the flower occurring as an ornament, or evidence of a disposition toward them, in many pictures of ladies. Rembrandt, for instance, to cite one out of endless examples, frequently uses a flower in this way, in his portraits of ladies, and among them the carnation; he twice depicts his wife, Saskia, holding one. The frontispiece, called "L'homme aux œillets," in a book by G. Geffroy, cited further on, is another example, and of a man. So, to take another instance, Mildred, Lady Burghley, in a portrait of her at Hatfield House, holds in her right hand a rose. It is unnecessary to cite further instances to prove what every one will admit. The heraldic import must have some other origin, and is not proved by the mere use of a flower in a picture. There is no heraldic significance in the custom, and not the slightest suggestion in it that a flower is especially adopted by a family. It is perhaps worth mention, though it seems very fanciful, that the carnation has not been given a definite meaning in the language of flowers, it at most sometimes taking the place of the rose, according at least to one authority (*The Floral Symbolism of the*

Great Masters, by Eliz. Haig, London, 1914). But the two girls might see a meaning for themselves in the arrangement of the flowers, as they were placed, and so, it is very likely, they did. The evidence from the flowers and leaves, then, in the double portrait, is distinctly contrary to the theory that the ladies in the portrait were sisters, or, both of them, members of the Fytton family.

In respect to the jewels, which are described by Mr. Bridgeman, as their description does not include those of Mary Fytton, with whom alone this Note is concerned, no attention need be paid to them here, except to mark that they are evidence of the wealth of the family. It might be supposed that the younger sister would have been allowed some jewel from the family jewel-box which might be recognized. Though her sister's jewels are recognized, and are connected by Mr. Bridgeman with jewels in other pictures, or with the family jewels, those of the lady on the right are not at all so connected, while they are conspicuous, especially in the second portrait, and therefore they seem to have been separate from the Fytton jewels, and denote the lady as of another family.

The inscription on the double portrait is: "ETATIS SUE 18. ANNO DOM 1592. ETATIS SUE 15," corre-

sponding nearly with the ages of Anne and Mary
Fytton. On examining the inscription, the first
impression of the spectator is of its unusualness,
the labels declaring the date of the painting and
the age of each of the young women, from which,
as this is a family portrait intended for continual
exhibition, the age of each of these technically
married but, in some degree, still free and unmarried girls could be told at any time, by any casual
visitor, a practise contrary to the custom of Englishmen, and rarely found anywhere, except in the case
of ladies of royal and therefore national prominence.
There are some other Sixteenth century portraits
at Arbury, some of which have more or less similar
Latin inscriptions; all are called collectively the
older portraits. Mr. Bridgeman's observations
upon these Latin inscriptions are as follows:

But besides these Eighteenth century inscriptions,
there are on several of the older pictures Latin words
and figures, giving the age of the subject of the portrait
and usually also the year in which it was painted; and
there seems no reason to doubt that these Latin
inscriptions are, as they obviously profess to be,
contemporaneous, and therefore entitled to credit. Details such as these could hardly have been added inno-
cently by a later generation; if not contemporaneous
they must be a deliberate attempt to mislead; and even
if so improbable an hypothesis could be entertained,
it is difficult to believe that with this object in view

any one would adopt so subtle a device as to give the date and age without any further clue to the name of the person depicted. . . . This picture [the double portrait], bears no Eighteenth century inscription, but at the top, in the middle, are the words "Anno dom 1592," in the left corner "Etatis sue 18," and in the right "Etatis sue 15."

Gossip from a Muniment Room; Appendix.

The "subtle device" suggested in the above quotation appears to stray from what is probable. It is unnecessary to imagine anything of such a kind. To say that "there seems no reason to doubt" these inscriptions, takes for granted what is contested, and applies to all of these inscriptions what may not be true of them all. The period of an inscription has been occasionally a matter of debate. Most of the inscriptions on the older portraits very likely were, as Mr. Bridgeman states, contemporaneous with the portraits on which they appear, though as no further photogravure has been published of them, there is no evidence to guide us. It does not, however, follow that in any particular instance the resemblance of one of these portraits to the others, in bearing an inscription, cannot be set aside, and the time of the inscription be shown to be later than the date which appears upon it. Such is the case of

Portrait in Court Dress, Claimed to be of Mary Fytton

the double portrait. It is maintainable that a mistake in one of the persons represented in the double portrait was made by the subsequent owners of Arbury, who then added the inscription to it. The possibility of such a mistake is established beyond cavil, if any proof of it can be necessary, by the attempt made at Arbury a century later than the indicated attempt with the double portrait, that is, in the Eighteenth century, to identify the portraits generally, then forming the gallery, when many mistakes were admittedly made, one of them, as it happened, occurring in one of the two portraits now in question, called of Mary Fytton, that in Court dress, which was then labelled as, "Lady Macclesfield, 3rd daughter of Sir Edw. Fitton, Dame of Honour to Q. Elizabeth," a lady who, as Mr. Bridgeman admits, never existed. A principle of evidence is put forward by Mr. Bridgeman in the course of his Appendix (p. 166), and the principle is valuable in respect to the evidence which is necessary to establish the contemporaneousness of the inscription with the double portrait, that as several of these Eighteenth century inscriptions are inaccurate, it would be unsafe to rely on the Eighteenth century inscriptions where they are not supported by independent evidence. The like principle holds

true of the inscription on the double portrait, that
if it shall appear that there is cause for a grave
doubt as to the period at which it was placed on
the portrait, its contemporaneousness with the
portrait cannot then be assumed, but must be
established by independent evidence, a principle
which should be remembered in coming to a conclusion as to this inscription. The date, 1768, has
been decided upon by Mr. Bridgeman as that of
the attempted identification of the portraits at
Arbury in the Eighteenth century. The time
when the earlier, and also mistaken, identification
of the double portrait might have taken place, and
which we think certainly occurred, and when the
mistake in the inscription would have followed,
might be the time of the Restoration, and the fifty
succeeding years, and possibly somewhat later,
though hardly earlier, than that. There is no
absence of a sufficient time in which a mistake
in the identification of the lady on the right in
the double portrait might have been made.

The precedents for the form used in the Latin
inscriptions at Arbury are numerous, and must
be given careful consideration. A series of miniatures by the younger Holbein, Nicholas Hilliard
and others, down through the time of the first
Stewart Kings, is still extant, and these artists, at

times, wrote on their miniatures inscriptions which have a perfect resemblance to the inscriptions at Arbury, giving the age of the subject of the miniature. Holbein often placed upon his easel portraits such inscriptions; other artists, coming from the Continent and then painting in London, also had, on occasion, this habit. Holbein's antecedents—he is considered usually to be the leader of the English school of miniaturists, and he was a remarkable painter of portraits—on his arrival in England in 1526, at the age of thirty-one years or over, had been of Basel and still more of the imperial city of Augsburg, where he and his father and his father-in-law and perhaps, though doubtfully, his grandfather, had been painters, and where he had probably placed an inscription of the kind on a portrait several years before his arrival in England. (*Holbein*, by Ralph N. Wornum, *passim*, pp. 48–99.) How far this unreticent and unnecessary habit was followed by native easel portrait painters, as it was in miniatures by Hilliard, it is difficult now to tell, as the instances are generally inaccessible, exhibitions of old family portraits by artists of minor ability being not as common as those of the contemporary miniatures. Few of them perhaps have survived to the present day as has the double portrait; the double portrait

shows little or no trace of Continental influence.
There are no English artists of the Sixteenth
century mentioned in the catalogue (1901), of the
National Portrait Gallery in London, except one
or two miniaturists; foreign influence was at that
time predominant in England. Mr. Wornum observes of the English artists: "Unfortunately
what our own Englishmen were we do not know,
but some of the respectable portraits of the period
must undoubtedly have been their work" (*ibid.*,
p. 201). The same view appears in an elaborate
discussion of the painters of this period in the
catalogue (illustrated), of the Burlington Fine
Arts Club's "Exhibition of Early English Portraiture" (1909). A list of these painters will be
found in *Anecdotes of Painting in England*, by
Horace Walpole (Wornum's ed., London, 1849,
vol. I, p. xxvii). The double portrait appears to
be a wholly local, perhaps provincial production,
excepting the inscription. Under what circumstances the inscription was placed upon the double
portrait at Arbury it is impossible to say positively,
and perhaps it will be better to wait until we see,
from a review of the more general evidence not
connected with the picture, what are the probabilities as to its date, rather than attempt any final
decision here. If the tendency of the other evi-

dence is to show that the double portrait does not contain a portrait of Mary Fytton, we are quite at liberty to believe that the inscription upon it was not placed upon it at the time when its date indicates, but rather at a later period. We should, however, first examine the accessible evidence bearing directly upon the inscription before leaving it, and see whether it may not in itself present a degree of doubt as to its contemporaneousness with the double portrait.

Upon a miniature, as much less public than an easel portrait, the inscription of date and age had a something personal and familiar to recommend it, and was not so plainly open to objection as when on an easel painting, though the practise, of which Holbein's are perhaps the earliest surviving instances in England, has not been continued. As miniatures bearing inscriptions of this kind have been extensively exhibited, catalogued and described, and are therefore easier of access than family portraits of native origin, their inscriptions can be studied with some approximation to thoroughness; if it appears that such an inscription as that on the double portrait was seldom used even on a miniature, that circumstance will cast a shade of doubt upon the contemporaneousness of the inscription with the double portrait.

Before entering upon this intricate matter, however, we will pause over a distinct question, the
seeming superfluity, not so much of flowers as of
leaves, in the double portrait, considered as the
portrait of the two Fytton sisters, that is, of the
obtrusive plant and leaf emblems on the sleeves
of the so-called Mary Fytton, and inquire besides
whether there was anything peculiar, not to easel
but to miniature art, a practise which might be
fancied to be separate from the art of easel portraits, to account for their presence. Inscriptions
of date and age, unlike floral decoration, were a
temporary and recent addition to the painter's art,
having been in use in 1592, as far as we have
noticed, about ninety-two years. On a miniature
of Queen Elizabeth by Hilliard, now in the National Portrait Gallery, London, the inscription is
"Anno Dni 1572, Ætatis Suæ 38." There is also
a crown with the letters "E. R.," and on the left
shoulder is a white rose, symbolical, no doubt, of
the Virgin Queen; if the rose were originally a
white and red Tudor rose it would denote the
Queen's family. A considerable number of miniatures, bearing this or a similar inscription, may be
found in the collections. The inference is plain,
and when reflecting upon the peculiar inscriptions
on the portraits at Arbury, certainly worth ex-

amination, that the inscription at Arbury followed the lettering upon some easel portrait or miniature of that type. Its resemblance to the inscription on the miniature is obvious. There can be no doubt that the inscription resembles in its terms the multitudinous class of inscriptions which figured upon current easel portraits and miniatures in the Sixteenth and Seventeenth centuries, though in its appearance, the arrangement of its lettering, it being more like a separate record or label, less like a part of the picture, as inscriptions were, more or less, usually made to be, it is a little different from any inscription which the writer has happened to observe. Precedents may be found for it, but it seems unlike most of the inscriptions of its date, and this is, perhaps, an important point. It is perhaps worth more attention than the writer, who is not at present near the European galleries, can give to it.

The flowers and leaves introduced into the double picture had, on the other hand, no particular origin in miniature art, but in the general principles of the art of both miniatures and easel portraits. Embellishments of such a kind are introduced in miniatures, when they occur, just as in other branches of Art, to meet the personal and special conditions or wishes of the subject

represented. An examination of the principal
books upon miniatures will disclose comparatively
few instances in which leafage or flowers were introduced, and in each of those cases it is evident—
as in the unique and well-known miniature of Mrs.
Pemberton, represented as holding a leaf—that
the flower or leaf was introduced for separate and
individual reasons, as it would be in any larger
painting, and not in pursuance of any fashion of
embellishment peculiar to miniature art, there not
being the least sign, in the great array of miniatures
illustrated or described, of the existence of any
special fashion of the kind. Flowers, indeed, were,
for some reason, perhaps of taste, perhaps because
of their excessive minuteness, or perhaps rather
as the result of a preference for jewels, relatively
little used in miniature, or much less than one
might expect in these "pictures in little." A
recent collection of miniatures, that of the late
John Pierpont Morgan, has been so elaborately
catalogued that statistics can be given of the use
of flowers in the miniatures of the time, within the
limits of that collection. The catalogue, vol. I
(1906), extending generally over the Sixteenth
and Seventeenth centuries, and listing about 175
miniatures, exhibits only about eight instances—of
which two are of gold, and one is painted with

golden leaves—of the use of flowers as embellishments of the dress or head-dress of the subject of
a miniature, showing that fashion did not tend in
miniature painting toward ornament by flowers.
Single leaves are used hardly anywhere, hardly in
any kind of painting, except in heraldry; the instance cited of Mrs. Pemberton's miniature is the
only one we happen to have met with or can recall.
In using the flowers and the leaves in the double
portrait, the artist acted of his own motion and
quite independently, that is to say, under the
general custom of artists, and not under any particular habit or tendency of miniaturists in that
direction. On an easel portrait we know that
flowers have been used from the beginning as
ornaments, as in truth they have on miniatures,
and also that this practise has not the remotest
connection with the transient custom of inscriptions.

The introduction of the leaves and flowers, then,
was probably due to some special request for them
by the two ladies themselves, and certainly the
lady on the right has a strange variety of them for
a daughter of the Fyttons, whose devices are not
said to include the holly and the palm, in addition
to the pansy. If it should be urged that those
devices might have included all three of these

symbols, it can be answered that in that case the lady would be quite unnecessarily and too much marked by them, and especially so for a younger daughter. The two symbols on her sleeves, if they have any meaning at all, and a meaning they must have had for her, establish her not as Mary Fytton but almost certainly as a member of another house. They were placed there by the painter, a little awkwardly as we see, by the lady's wish, and seemingly to distinguish her family from that of the Fyttons whose pansy she carried in her bouquet. The presence of the two leaves, the holly and the palm, in the absence of any evidence to contradict their testimony, goes a great way toward proof that the lady on the right was not the younger daughter, Mary Fytton, but a distinct person, and not a member of the house of Fytton. Anne's residence at the time, and the migration of the portrait with her from her girlhood's home at Gawsworth to Arbury, will be noticed in another place.

What, then, should we think of the crucial problem of the Arbury portraits, the question of the true date of the inscription on the double portrait; whether that it was attached at the time when the portrait was painted, or that it was added at a later period? We have seen that there is more than one reason to doubt that the lady on the right represents a younger sister of the lady on the left, which casts of necessity the like doubt upon the date of the inscription. The inscription on the portrait is in the precise words used by miniaturists and the painters of larger portraits not only then but for more than half a century afterwards, through the first half and, to some extent, still later in the Seventeenth century. Miniatures with this inscription, though of a departed fashion, existed in relatively considerable numbers at the termination of the Seventeenth century, as did the more important easel portraits, and this style of inscription was familiar to all persons interested in them, while at Arbury itself there were several easel portraits bearing it and frequently seen by the owner. An elucidation of the evidence, impalpable as an historical hypothesis necessarily is, may be hazarded; it can never be proved, but it still corresponds exactly with the condition in which the portraits are now found. We may infer, then, from what we have already ascertained as to the double portrait, that not only the second or single portrait, but also the double portrait was, when it was painted, without an inscription, and that in the time of the Restoration, perhaps of the Revolution or of Queen Anne, the owner of Arbury,

Sir Richard Newdigate, the honourable and patriotic Judge, or perhaps his widow or his descendant, wishing to make permanent their understanding of the two pictures, perhaps hesitating over Mary's name already legendary and unsuited to any display on a family portrait, and thinking the double portrait to be a portrait of the two sisters, chose to follow the recently disused Latin form of identifying portraits, which habitually left the name unstated and a matter of inference, which already existed on the other older portraits at Arbury, and which was appropriate to a portrait of its time, and that they used it on the double portrait only, leaving the second and single portrait in Court dress wholly unlabelled, considering that to be of the same person as was the lady on the right in the double portrait, and deeming any further identification of it neither necessary nor desirable. That the second Sir Richard Newdigate, presumably a son of Judge Newdigate who died in 1678, was interested in the family genealogy in 1686 appears from a note to Mr. Bridgeman's Appendix to Lady Newdegate's book, at page 172. This interest may have been connected with family litigation between two other branches of the Fytton descendants, but it existed, and shows, in the nature of Sir Richard's observation, the frequent shortness of family memory in respect to even immediate connections, if such connections were not members of the same household or of the same neighbourhood. We disregard, of course, the inscription placed in the Eighteenth century upon the single portrait.

It seems quite plain that only by some such hypothesis of a subsequent addition of the inscription, can the divergence of the inscription from the double portrait itself be explained, for the inscription, which seems to refer to the two Fytton sisters, is not confirmed in the details of the portrait, nor by the likenesses of the two ladies themselves. We should reflect, also, that there was no period in 1592, the date inscribed on the portrait, when the girls could be called accurately 18 and 15 years old respectively, as Mary's fifteenth birthday did not come until June, 1593; the mistake in the inscription would be more likely to come in a subsequent identification of the picture than at the time when it was painted.

There is no noticeable difficulty in the theory that the inscription was subsequent to the portrait, that it was mistaken, and that it was placed on the portrait at the end of the Seventeenth, rather than at the end of the Sixteenth century. Perhaps an objection could be made to the selection by the subsequent owner of a particular year, 1592, as the date for the picture. Still, an owner wishing to establish some date, as he very properly would wish to do, and we know, too, that the other older portraits at Arbury were, for the most part, dated, might venture to approximate to it, for it cannot be far from correct in respect to Anne, who was to him the principal person in the picture. She was his respected ancestress, while the unfortunate Mary was less than no one, a blot in the family pedigree. No year, as the present writer views the picture, will reconcile the known ages of the two Fytton sisters with the apparent ages of the two girls in the double portrait, because if the date is postponed to suit Mary's likeness, it becomes too late for her sister. If he chose the year when Anne was eighteen, which corresponds well with her appearance in the portrait, he might decline to consider the supposed and unvalued Mary at all, noticing merely her mature appearance by giving her the greatest possible age consistent with the age he had first selected for Anne, and calling her fifteen instead of the fourteen and a half, or a little over, which was her age at the end of 1592. He probably would not be interested in, or curious or careful as to her, indeed the contrary rather, and would prefer to consider Anne alone, in dating the picture. Perhaps the story of Anne's life-long faithfulness to her sister had some connection with the origin and strength of the belief that the lady with her in the portrait was her sister, Mary Fytton. Nothing, however, is more certain in respect to this portrait than that some one erred in the inscription, and whether our attempt to explain the condition of the picture is in accordance with common probability and the frequent forgetfulness and uncertainty of families as to old portraits, or not, the error was one which would more probably be made by a subsequent owner, bent upon identifying the portrait, than by the people interested when the portrait was painted. The date of Anne's baptism is 6th October 1574, Mary's 24th June 1578. Mary became fifteen years of age on, or near to, June 24th, 1593, not 1592. It is contrary to the commonest experience to think that such a mistake as that would be made when a formal family portrait, as this would have been if it had been of the two sisters, was painted, and the ladies whose portraits were taken were present. Mr. Bridgeman has noticed this weakness in the inscription, as his interpretation of the inscription is too strained to be admissible for a moment, and shows how difficult he has thought a defence of the inscription in this direction to be. His understanding of the inscription is that the figures, 18 and 15, mean that the girls were then not eighteen and fifteen years old, but in their eighteenth and fifteenth years respectively. It is a forlorn hope to ascribe to an inscription a meaning which is contrary to common sense, the common meaning of language, and all precedent. If the painter intended by his inscription to convey to the reader that the ladies were in their eighteenth and fifteenth years, he wrote it in terms which, according to the customary use of language, have no relation to his intention and convey a different impression. Eighteen and fifteen mean in the inscription what they mean in every legal document and in every common conversation, that is, the attainment of those ages. The painter did not say what Mr. Bridgeman suggests that he said.

It is perhaps worth while to add also, as it brings out the error in the inscription more strikingly by showing its extent, that it is unusual to state as a lady's age one at which she has not yet arrived. Mr. Bridgeman's limitation of the time within which the inscription was so peculiarly written, to the period between June and October in 1592, makes this lapse from the common conventionality happen in the case of both sisters, that is, if the painter meant what he wrote, as we are bound to believe that he did. If the painter added the inscription when Mr. Bridgeman supposes him to have done so, that is, between Anne's birthday and Mary's birthday, or between October and June in 1592, both the girls' ages would be anticipated by the artist, Anne's by a little time, but Mary's by from eight and a half to twelve months, a proceeding which would hardly be accepted by the families of the young ladies, and still less by themselves. Mr. Bridgeman's explanation is:

Anne Fitton was baptized at Gawsworth, 6th October, 1574, Mary Fitton 24th June, 1578, so that, if the picture was painted between the months of June and October, 1592, their ages would exactly correspond with those given on the picture, one being then in her eighteenth, the other in her fifteenth year.

Gossip from a Muniment Room. Appendix.

This is a pure assumption that the painter of the portrait took an unusual course, and also one that would be ambiguous and misleading, in stating the ages of the two young ladies. The inscription is in the ordinary form, and it presumably has the ordinary meaning, and there is no reason whatever why it should be supposed that it was intended to be understood otherwise. It is impossible to follow Mr. Bridgeman when he says (p. 169), that the probability that the portrait is of two sisters is confirmed "by the exact correspondence of the age of the younger girl as recorded on the picture, with that of Mary Fitton in 1592." It would be nearer the fact to say that this probability is much lessened by the unquestionable inaccuracy of the inscription in this respect; such correspondence, as Mr. Bridgeman terms it, is not that which is usual, nor would it be tolerable, in the record of a family portrait. Mr. Bridgeman's silence as to this view of the inscription shows the extent of his difficulty.

The testimony of the inscription itself, then, is, we have reason for holding, contrary to the theory that it was a part of the picture in 1592, and this testimony is supported by the appearance of the ladies themselves in the portrait, and by several of its details. It will be admitted, on looking over the evidence collected in various parts of this Note, that the further indirect testimony, which can be brought against the contemporaneousness of the inscription with the picture, is worth much consideration; the evidence for it appears to be no more than its presence on the picture, and its long and unquestioned acceptance by the owners of Arbury.

Before leaving this phase of the inscription, it should be observed that the legend inscribed on

the portrait which forms the frontispiece of Lady
Newdegate's book, stating Mary's age as 15, is not
only not justified by the inscription, but that it is
not supported even by Mr. Bridgeman's construc-
tion of it.

To enter now upon the question, whether the inscription is found commonly on miniatures, or on
family portraits, it is particularly worth considering whether any artist, even a miniaturist, had he
worked on the picture, would have made ascertainable, and at any period, and by any casual
visitor, these young women's ages, through their
permanent and semi-public portrait, at the time of
its painting. We think it next to impossible that
this should have been done, and we will examine,
therefore, the record of inscription writing to determine whether painters, by any possibility, were
in the habit of making inscriptions of this kind.
The question is worth an examination, for if we
should see that the inscription was, if not contrary
to any consciously defined rule, at least not customary and, in practise, very unusual, that would
go some distance toward proving that the inscription was a subsequent addition to the double
portrait.

It is true that one or both of the sisters had

been, at the time, technically married, but, living at home, and subject only to a childhood contract of marriage, which seems in the case of the younger, if it existed, to have been disapproved and broken off, and in the case of the elder, to have not been carried out until some years after the double portrait had been painted, they should be regarded as if still free and unmarried girls, that is, for the purposes of the inscription, as in respect to their future, practically, and subject to the direction of their parents, they still remained.

The records show that an inscription of the kind was but seldom placed upon miniatures, and that there is no similar and certain case, so far as we are aware, among easel portraits, excepting in royal circles. If it proves to have been exceptional upon the more familiar form of the miniature, an inference must arise against its contemporaneousness with the double portrait, and if no clear and certain instance of it appears among easel portraits, that inference must be greatly strengthened. It should be admitted, at the outset, that the question of the existence of any such rule for the portraits of young ladies as is suggested, is not free from evident difficulty, much confusion inhering in the evidence, consisting as it does of a multitude of unrelated and independent instances, of which often no knowledge survives but what they themselves afford. The substantial unanimity, under these difficult circumstances, of the records examined is surprising, when it is considered that this was, after all, only an instinctive and habitual, and not at all an enforced rule, there being an almost entire absence from the examined records of clear and unmistakable instances similar to the double portrait, and not so frequent instances as to which a doubt will arise as to make them important through their number.

In miniatures, an assured precedent for the inscription is very rare; we have happened to find in the records, so far as we have seen them, only one which is certain; there are a few which are uncertain. There are precedents of royal miniatures, and also of royal easel portraits, but in those cases the age of the lady might be considered to be so publicly known as to make the inscription indifferent to the lady as well as of interest to the public. It is not possible, desirable as it is, to make a statement of all the evidence given by miniatures, no complete description of them existing and we will restrict ourselves, therefore, to the books at hand. An analysis of vol. i of the Morgan catalogue of miniatures, mentioned hitherto, in which each miniature is carefully described, and as to which exact statistics can be had, gives the following examples only of miniatures with the complete inscription of the date of the miniature and of the then age of the subject, such as that on the double portrait, and from which the age of the person represented can be at any moment told:

MARY, QUEEN OF SCOTS, by an unknown artist, (p. 45). Inscription: Maria Scotorum Regina, 1565, Aetat. XXIII.

LADY HUNSDON, by N. Hilliard, (p. 26): Ano Dm 1576, Eais suae 25.

COUNTESS OF PEMBROKE, by N. Hilliard, (p. 35): Ano 157 (?) Aet. 29.

EARL OF SUSSEX, by N. Hilliard (p. 39): Ano Dm 15 (?) Aetatis suae 36.

MARY, QUEEN OF SCOTS, by N. Hilliard, (p. 29): Anno Dom 1581, Aetatis suae (?).

LORD BROOKE, by Isaac Oliver, (p. 54): Ano Dm 1588, Aetatis suae 22.

GENTLEMAN, the artist unknown, (p. 73): Anno Domini 1588, Etatis suae 19.

SIR H. FANSHAWE, by Isaac Oliver, (p. 61): Ano Dm 1608, Aeta. 43.

ANNE, QUEEN OF JAMES I, by Isaac Oliver, (p. 59): Ano Dm 1609, Aetatis suae 28.

EARL OF ESSEX, by Isaac Oliver, (p. 52): Aetatis suae (?) 1614.

RHYS GRIFFITHS, by Isaac Oliver, (p. 56): Ano Domi 1617, Aetatis suae 55.

LADY, the School of Oliver, (p. 68): 1619 (?) Aet. 28 (?).

EARL OF SOMERSET, by Peter Oliver, (p. 67): Aetat. (?) A. D. 1623.

GENTLEMAN, by L. Hilliard, (p. 63): Ano Dni 1640, Aetatis suae 75 (?).

DUKE OF BERWICK, by the younger Hoskins, (p. 86): engraved inscription on the reverse, Aet. 29, 1700.

No case appears in the list of a young girl whose miniature is inscribed as in the double portrait, though the system of inscribing miniatures then was at its height. As the matrimonial *status* of the lady in the miniature of 1619 is not known, the instance is doubtful; the numerals upon it, given by Dr. Williamson, the editor of the catalogue, are not perfectly decipherable.

The age of the subject, but omitting the date of the painting, appears sometimes upon a miniature, and is less objectionable:

ARNOLD FRANZ, by Holbein, (p. 7): Aet. 32.
MRS. PEMBERTON, by Holbein, (p. 8): Anno Etatis suae 23.

The date of the miniature, but not the age of the subject, occurs often:

LADY, by Levina Teerlinc, (p. 21): Ano Dm 15 (?).
"LA BELLE SOURDIS," by N. Hilliard, (p. 31): Ano Dm 1577.
LA PRINCESSE DE CONDÉ, by N. Hilliard, (p. 33): 1597.

To these last succeeds, in the general history of miniatures, the unended series in which the date alone of the miniature is given.

Dr. George C. Williamson's *History of Portrait Miniatures* (1904), names a very great number of them, but they necessarily are not always described individually, as in his more limited editing of the Morgan catalogue, many being grouped, and mentioned by name and place only, and exact statistics of these cannot therefore be given; the greater part of them, no doubt, have appeared in the exhibition catalogues. The general inference from them is the same as that from the Morgan collection, and no certainly young and single lady, in private life, is mentioned in the book, and her miniature described, whose age is defined as in the double portrait. Instances from Dr. Williamson's book which border on relevance to the inscription on the double portrait are:

The wife of Nicholas Hilliard, by him (vol. i, p. 17). An attractive miniature of his wife, more valuable through its exact labelling, with the inscription in a circle around the frame: "Alicia Brandon Nicolai Hilliardi qui propria manu depinxit uxor prima Ano Dni 1578 Aetatis suae 22," and the initials N. H.

Mrs. Holland, Maid of Honour to Queen Elizabeth, by Isaac Oliver (p. 32): Aetatis suae 27.

The Elector Palatine and his family by Alexander Cooper (p. 78). A series of twelve royal miniatures, showing the dates of painting and also the ages of the individuals. Dr. Williamson says of them that they belong to the German Emperor, and that "They are a series of circular miniatures, each set in an enamel frame and folding one over the other." He also says: "at the back of each portrait, in the same coloured enamel, is the name and age of the person whose portrait is contained in the disc, and the date (also recorded) when it was painted. . . . In the centre of the series is the portrait of Frederick V., Elector Palatine, and afterwards King of Bohemia, inscribed: Frederick R. B. Aet. 36, 16 August 1632. By his side is a portrait of his wife, Elizabeth, daughter of James I of England: Elizabeth R. B. Aetat. 36, 9 August 1632, the famous Queen of Hearts." The remaining miniatures of the series, all similarly inscribed, represented the ten children of the royal pair, four of them daughters. Of the youngest, Sophia, Aetat. 2, 14 Octobris 1633, "we have no portrait, and this is peculiarly unfortunate, as to Englishmen she is the most interesting of the series, for after flirting with a Portuguese grandee, an Italian duke, a Swedish prince, and her cousin Charles of England, she married the Elector Ernest of Hanover, and became the ancestress of the Hanoverian sovereigns, and of the dynasty which now occupies the throne of England."

In another of Dr. Williamson's publications, *How to Identify Portrait Miniatures* (1904), is an illustration of two little girls, aged respectively four and five years, whose ages are inscribed, with the date of painting. The four princesses, daughters of the Elector Palatine, and the miniature of Queen Elizabeth in the National Portrait Gallery, hereinabove mentioned, are excepted by the royal station of the ladies from the custom; besides these, the instances noticed in the books so far cited of a portrait miniature of any young, unmarried lady, giving at once the date of painting and the lady's age, are the uncertain case in 1619, in the Morgan collection, of an unknown lady aged twenty-eight, whose marriage is not stated or ascertainable, and the case just mentioned of the two little children still in their infancy.

So far as the question before us can be decided from the three books referred to, the case against the inscription on the double portrait, that it was contrary to the common practice of miniaturists, and therefore still less to be expected upon an easel portrait, has little opposition, but by going further afield a few difficult miniatures have been found which it is necessary to examine. Some other books consulted are by Dr. Williamson, Dr. Propert, Joshua J. Foster and Dudley Heath; some catalogues have also been examined, namely: "Early English Portrait Miniatures in the Collection of the Duke of Buccleuch," Montague House (in *The Studio*, 1917); "The Welbeck Abbey Miniatures belonging to his Grace the Duke of Portland" (in the fourth annual volume of the Walpole Society, 1914–15); Catalogue of an Exhibition of Miniatures by the Burlington Fine Arts Club (London, 1889); and the Miniature section in a catalogue of an Exhibition of Early English Portraiture, by the same Club (London, 1909).

The perhaps single, clear exception, and one to

which allusion has already been made, an exception unique in the books examined, to the observance that unmarried ladies, not in the royal circle, should not have their ages coupled with the date of painting and placed upon their miniatures, occurs in a list mentioned by Mr. Foster in one of his volumes, *Miniature Painters, British and Foreign*, vol. i, p. 34 (London, 1903), thus: "Mrs. Holland, Maid of Honour, dated 1593, Aetatis suae 26," by Nicholas Hilliard.

This miniature, as it happened, was followed in the next year by one by Isaac Oliver of the same lady, with an abbreviated inscription, and made in comparison unobjectionable by the omission of the date, "Aetatis suae 27." There is no illustration or description in Mr. Foster's volume of the earlier of the two miniatures, but it is probably that illustrated by Dr. Propert in his *History of Miniature Art* (1887), on the plate facing page 58. The later miniature is illustrated by Dr. Williamson, in his *History of Portrait Miniatures*, Plate XII and page 32. Each is an interesting miniature. The reflection at once necessarily occurs that there may have been a mistake about the earlier inscription, · as it can hardly have been placed on the miniature with the young lady's understanding or by her wish; at all events, it was not repeated on the second miniature. Unquestionably, the precedent is unlikely to attract a young lady of today, who might wish to make use of a miniature of herself among her friends. A third miniature, called of Mistress Holland, and again by Nicholas Hilliard, which, if of the same lady, was taken much later, and probably after marriage, and when she had become Lady Cope, will be found in the Morgan catalogue, vol. i, Pl. XIX and p. 39; this has no inscription. To illustrate more particularly the distinction between the two classes of inscription: in the catalogue of the Burlington Fine Arts Club of 1909, two miniatures ascribed to Holbein and of royal ladies are mentioned; one is of Queen Jane Seymour, inscribed, "An. XXV" (p. 114), and the other of Queen Katherine Parr, inscribed, "Ano. XXXII" (p. 117); neither is dated, and they are irrelevant to the double portrait, the ladies being neither unmarried nor in a private station, but they aid in illustrating the point that an inscription in the limited form placed on the second miniature of Mistress Holland, and of those of the two Queens has not the inconvenience and unfitness of the inscription placed on the earlier miniature of Mistress Holland, nor of that on the double portrait, for as the date of the miniature is omitted, a continuous statement is avoided of the precise age at any future moment of the lady represented.

In addition, a few doubtful miniatures appear in the catalogues, and they need careful and studious attention. To the catalogue of the Duke of Buccleuch's miniatures is annexed a catalogue of an exhibition of miniatures at the Victoria and Albert Museum, in which the following instances are mentioned of the miniatures of unknown ladies:

"A Lady unknown, in her 18th Year. Dated 1592." By Nicholas Hilliard or Isaac Oliver.

"A Lady unknown, in her 19th Year, Represented as Lucretia. Dated 1608." By Nicholas Hilliard.

"A Lady unknown, in her 52nd Year. Dated 1572." By Nicholas Hilliard.

These seem to be mentioned among the Welbeck Abbey miniatures, in the catalogue of that collection at pages 34 and 35, without further information as to them except that the lady described as Lucretia is holding a dagger. Lucretia is mentioned in Shakspeare's poem, then much in vogue, as the wife of Collatinus; a young spinster might take it upon herself to represent the injured lady, but the portrait is at least as likely to be of a lady who was herself married. The incident was frequently represented in portraits at that time. The miniature of a lady in her eighteenth year is per-

haps that mentioned with a slight variation—
there being frequently difficulty in reading the
inscriptions, the date being 1572 instead of 1592—
in the Burlington Fine Arts Club's catalogue (1909)
of Early English Portraiture, at page 124, the
description of the miniature being otherwise the
same. Let us admit them to be distinct miniatures.
The instance of the lady aged fifty-two years may
be disregarded, as she had passed beyond the age
to which the rule applies.

In the extensive catalogue of the miniatures exhibited by the Burlington Fine Arts Club in 1889,
is an entry on page 130:

"PORTRAIT OF A LADY. DATED 1600. AETATIS 23."

No further information appears in the catalogue
in respect to this miniature. The extent, therefore,
of the questionable instances among miniatures,
found in the books and catalogues hitherto cited,
and in some slight degree contravening a presumed
recognition in the Sixteenth and Seventeenth centuries of a reticence founded on natural sentiments,
and which would at the present day be generally
respected, is five, of unknown ladies aged 18, 18,
19, 23 and 28. The uncertainty as to these miniatures deprives them of clear value as evidence; the
probabilities as to them depend upon the ultimate

answer to the proposed question, whether there was in fact a habit of courtesy in existence in respect to the miniatures and larger portraits of young and unmarried ladies; if there was such a custom, then the miniatures were more probably inscribed in accordance with it, and were of young matrons. It has been said that marriage was at that period customarily earlier than it is now, and less often omitted. We will leave the question then as to these unidentified miniatures in suspense, to look further into the practice of the artists of the time; the remarkable absence from the records of a class of identified miniatures of young ladies clearly opposing the custom is of too much weight to be negatived by a few uncertain miniatures, doubtful as one or two of them may seem to be.

Since writing the preceding pages, two further catalogues have come to our hands, and they will be noticed now separately, the "Catalogue of the Special Exhibition of Portrait Miniatures on loan at the South Kensington Museum, June, 1865," extending to 3081 examples, and the illustrated "Catalogue of a collection of Miniatures in Plumbago, etc.," lent by Francis Wellesley, Esq., Victoria and Albert (South Kensington) Museum (London, 1915). The latter interesting catalogue contains nothing open to question, though it has several inscriptions, but the former adds two to the number of unknown young women whose miniatures bear both their ages and the date of the painting; on the other hand, it adds no further instance to the first miniature of Mistress Holland, which appears in its pages. This catalogue adds also a child of five years and a girl of six to the instances of the two little girls of four and five years old, whose miniatures were inscribed with date of painting and their ages, as already noticed. The examples of miniatures of unidentified young women are:

Page 99. "PORTRAIT OF A LADY, DATED ANNO 1600, AETATIS 23," by an unknown artist.
Page 179. "PORTRAIT OF A LADY IN A CLOSE CAP AND SMALL RUFF. INSCRIBED ANO DNI 1575, AETATIS SUAE 25," by an unknown artist.
Page 238. "PORTRAIT OF A LADY. AETATIS SUAE 20. ANO DNI 1587," by an unknown artist.

Of these, the first has, no doubt, been mentioned already from the Burlington Club's catalogue of 1889, but the second and third have not, and may be either the miniatures of young wives or of spinsters. The current of the evidence is so decided, however, toward establishing the existence of the common custom as to the portraits of spinsters, as will appear to any searcher through the extensive books and catalogues, that the miniatures of this uncertain kind can be tentatively, at least, as-

sumed to be the miniatures of married ladies, or
else to be exceptions to the common practice. The
two children's miniatures listed in the catalogue
are:

Page 186. "PORTRAIT OF A CHILD IN A RICHLY QUILTED DRESS,
WITH THE INSCRIPTION: ANNO DNI 1578, AETATIS 5," by
Nicholas Hilliard.
Page 240. "MARGARITA GONZAGA. INSCRIBED: MARGARITA
GONZAGA, ANNORUM VI, XIII MAII, MDLXXI," by Paolo
Veronese.

The first of these is of unstated sex, but the
second is of an additional little girl, whose miniature has been given an especially complete inscription. The inscriptions for feminine children, like
those for ladies past the age of courtship, depart
from the strictness of the convention, and indicate
the limits of the customary courtesy. Such, and
no more, are the difficult instances of miniatures
which have been found in the books and catalogues
cited.

Turning from miniatures to easel or family portraits, our search through a representative selection
of the books and catalogues likely to contain evidence, has discovered but few cases of doubt as to
the observance of the rule of courtesy to unmarried
ladies, and no identified and certain infraction of it.
The fashion, alike unnecessary and inconvenient

in practice, of inscribing on the front of a portrait the age of the person represented, commenced, as far as we have noticed, with the first year of the Sixteenth century, and continued through the century and thereafter for the greater part of the Seventeenth century; it began to fade during the Commonwealth, and died out almost wholly during the reign of Charles II. A considerable number of the existing portraits bear inscriptions of this kind, either of the age of the subject joined with the date of painting, or of the age of the subject and having the date of the painting omitted. A list of the books and catalogues examined is:

TEXT-BOOKS

Raphael, by Crowe and Cavalcaselle. (London, 1882–5.)
Titian, by the same authors. (London, 1877.)
History of Painting in North Italy, by the same authors; 2d ed. (London, 1912.)
Italian Painters, by G. Morelli. (London, 1892–3.)
Notes on the Brera Gallery at Milan, by Charles Locke Eastlake (1883.)
Notes on the Royal Gallery at Venice, by the same author. (1888.)
Holbein, by Ralph N. Wornum. (London, 1867.)
Anecdotes of Painting in England, by Horace Walpole; ed. R. N. Wornum. (London, 1849.)
Tour of a German Artist in England, with Notices of Private Galleries, by Johann David Passavant. (London, 1836.)
Treasures of Art in Great Britain, by Dr. Gustav Friedrich Waagen. (London, 1854.)
Les Musées d'Europe; Berlin, the Kaiser Friedrich Museum, by Gustave Geffroy. (Paris, 1910.)

CATALOGUES

The National Gallery. (London, 1899.)

The National Portrait Gallery. (London, 1901.)

The Burlington Fine Arts Club; Exhibition of Early English Portraiture. (London, 1909.)

Musée National du Louvre. Notice des Tableaux exposés; Écoles d'Italie, Écoles d'Espagne, Écoles Allemande, Flamande et Hollandaise, et École Française, par Frédéric Villot. (Paris, 1872.)

The Louvre; Italian and Spanish Schools, by the Vte Both de Tauzia. (Paris, 1885.)

Description raisonnée des Peintures du Louvre. Tome I, Écoles Étrangères, Italie et Espagne, par Seymour de Ricci. (Paris, 1913.) The further volumes of this catalogue if they have yet been published, have not been accessible.

Exhibition by the Alsace-Lorraine Society at Paris. (Nearly 600 pictures. 1874.)

The Uffizi Gallery. (Florence; C. Rigoni, 1886.)

The Gallery of the Pitti Palace. (Florence; E. Chiavacci, 1875.)

Siena; Accademia. (1872.)

Venice; Accademia di Belli Arti. (1885.)

The same Gallery, by A. Conti. (1895.)

Modena; Reale Galleria Estense. (1854.)

Bologna; Reale Pinacoteca. (1883.)

Milan; Palazzo di Brera, Pinacoteca. (1892.)

Berlin; Königliche Museen. (G. F. Waagen, 1860.)

Vienna; Gemälde der Belvedere-Galerie. (1882–6.)

Dresden; Königliche Gemälde-Galerie. (1912.)

Munich; Paintings in the Old Pinakothek; trans. J. T. Clarke. (1885.)

The Complete work of Rembrandt, by Dr. Wilhelm Bode, trans. Florence Simmonds. 8 vols. fo., illustrated. (Paris, 1897–1906.)

The Metropolitan Museum of Art, New York. (1905.)

The same. Loan Exhibition of Paintings by old Dutch Masters; Hudson-Fulton Exhibition. (1909.)

These books record a great number of portraits of ladies, and some of their portraits bear inscrip-

tions; those inscriptions which most nearly approach the inscription on the double portrait have
been selected for examination, and are as follows:

INSTANCES FROM TEXT-BOOKS

"Titian," by Crowe and Cavalcaselle

In the second volume of Crowe and Cavalcaselle's
Titian, at page 68, a portrait by Titian of a ten-
year-old girl is described, with its inscription of
date and age. "On a tablet high up on the wall to
the left" is inscribed: "Annor. X, MDXLII," and,
"on the edge of a console to the right" appears
"Titianus F." In respect to this inscription, the
writer has seen a reproduction of the picture, and
thinks that Titian made use of the inscription as
an artistic accessory in carrying out his conception of the portrait; genuine inscriptions are often
combined with, or made to enter into the picture,
to a greater or lesser extent. There is apparently
an error by the distinguished authors in their
statement of the inscription. The picture is
called a portrait of a daughter of Roberto Strozzi.
Such a portrait of a daughter of Roberto Strozzi,
exactly similar to the description given above,
and in all points to what else is said eloquently
of the picture by Messrs. Crowe and Cavalcaselle
is reproduced as a full-page illustration in *Les
Musées d'Europe, Berlin, Kaiser Friedrich Museum*
(Paris, 1910), by Gustave Geffroy, to face page
140, in which the age of the subject appears on the
tablet as two, not ten, "Annor. II," not Annor. X,

and the lesser age is established by the appearance of the child herself. When described by Messrs. Crowe and Cavalcaselle, the picture was in the Palazzo Strozzi at Florence, but it has since appeared in the catalogue of the "Königliche Museen zu Berlin am Lustgarten " (Berlin, W. Spemann, 1902), and it is there said of it (p. 83), "das des Töchterchens des Roberto Strozzi," and at page 93, "Bildniss einer Tochter des Roberto Strozzi aus Florenz (1542)." This date is that inscribed on the tablet in the picture, and for this reason, and the coincidence in description, it is the same picture as that mentioned by Messrs. Crowe and Cavalcaselle, and their statement of the age of the child is not correct.

At the end of Messrs. Crowe and Cavalcaselle's volumes is a list, covering 38 pages, of uncertified or spurious pictures ascribed to Titian, among which occurs, at page 447, an unauthentic portrait of a little girl, inscribed: "Aetatis Suae 4 nel Maio. Per Titiano e fatto a Cadoro, 1518." This portrait and the preceding genuine portrait by Titian should be classed with the miniatures of the little girls of 4, 5 and 6 years old, mentioned heretofore, in which the strict convention is laid aside.

"History of Painting in North Italy"

Portrait of a nun at the Accademia in Venice. A footnote describes the painting as: "Bust on a light ground of a nun with her left hand on her bosom, inscribed on the ground and above two escutcheons, F. A. XLVIII A. A. XV." If we may

8

attempt to interpret this inscription, it seems to
mean that the portrait is of a lady in her sixteenth
year (unless, perhaps, the numerals denoting her
age are also contracted), and painted in 1548, but
as it was connected with her taking the vows, it
is hardly relevant here. (Vol. iii, p. 188.)

Portrait of a lady in a red dress and with a book in
her hand, standing with her elbow on a pier,
and painted by Bernardino Licinio. Inscription:
"1540. Die 25 Feb." The picture is merely
dated, and this, as it gives no age for the lady, is
not an inscription in the sense in which we use the
term. (Vol. iii, p. 189.)

"Italian Painters," by G. Morelli

Portrait of the artist herself by a feminine artist,
Sofonisba Anguissola. The portrait is said to be
in the Collection of Portraits at the Uffizi in
Florence, and is inscribed: "Sophonisba Anguissola, Cremis, Aet. Suae Ann. XX," but it has no
date. A picture of the Holy Family by this lady,
now in the gallery at Bergamo, is inscribed:
"Sophonisba Anagussola, (sic), Adolescens, P.
1559," but is not a portrait, and does not give a
definite age for the painter. (Vol. i, p. 198.)

The inscription on a portrait belonging to Lady Eastlake, by Cordegliaghi, is said to be: "X 1504,
Andreas Cordelle Agy, discipulus johannis bel-
lini pinxit 24." (Vol. ii, p. 237.) The "24" is
said to be not a statement of age but the "monogram" of the painter (History of Painting in North
Italy, vol. i, p. 280, note); the picture is described
by Dr. Waagen in his notices of English private

galleries (vol. ii, p. 265), as not a portrait but a "Marriage of St. Catherine."

"Holbein" by R. N. Wornum

In the large family picture of the family of Sir Thomas More, a picture not now in existence and perhaps never wholly completed, but preserved through a sketch and in several dissimilar copies, the ages and the names of the persons introduced seem to have been inscribed throughout by Holbein; the ladies in the picture were, however, either married or betrothed.   Compare with this the instances of pictures of assembled families found in *Anecdotes of Painting*, by Horace Walpole (*infra*), and in the Dresden and Berlin catalogues.   No certainly genuine date for Holbein's original picture appears to exist, the date, 1530, on his sketch being a later addition.   (Pages 229, 235, 243.)

The Berlin Museum contains a small picture of a Queen Anne, called Anne Boleyn, and perhaps by Holbein (page 269).   Inscription: "Anna Regina, 1525, Anno Aetatis 22."   The portrait is considered to be a likeness of the royal lady, but as Anne Boleyn was not married to Henry VIII until 1532, the inscription is evidently a subsequent addition to the portrait, resembling in this respect, as we think, the inscription on the double portrait.   Moreover, its statement of the Queen's age seems more likely than that of Camden, the annalist, which differs from it.   Mr. Wornum doubts the picture being a work by Holbein; it is attributed to Holbein, however, in the Museum's catalogue.

"Anecdotes of Painting," by Horace Walpole

"In the Palace at Kensington are two daughters of Philip II of Spain. 1. Isabella Clara, fil. Phil. II. Regis Hisp. aet. 11, 1571. 2. Catherine, aet. 10." The painter was Sir Anthony More; the young ladies, even later on, as royal personages, were doubtless careless of the inscription. (Vol. i, p. 143.)

A picture of an assembled family, painted by Lucas de Heere. "An elderly gentleman is at table with his wife and another lady, probably, from the resemblance, her sister. Before them are seven young children, their ages marked, which show that three of them were born at a birth." No date for this picture is mentioned; it is said to represent the family of Sir George Brooke, Lord Cobham, and should be classed with the portrait of the family of Sir Thomas More, just noted, and with the Hibbard, Mytens, and one unnamed family-assemblage pictures, referred to further on. (Vol. i, p. 156.)

A portrait of Anne of Denmark, Queen of James I, painted by Paul Van Somer. Inscription: "Anna Reg. &c., Aet. 43." Whether the portrait has a date is not stated, but, representing a royal and also married lady, it does not come within the convention. (Vol. i, p. 210.)

A portrait of five of the children of Charles I, by Sir Anthony Vandyck. Inscription: "Regis Magnae Brittaniae proles. Princ. Carolus, nat. 29 May, 1630; Jac. D. Ebor. nat. 14 Oct. 1633; Princpssa Maria, nat. 4 Nov. 1631; Princip. Eliza, nat. 28 Dec. 1635; Princip. Anna, nat. 17 May, 1637;

Ant. Vandyck Eq., fecit, 1637." The inscription of these dates, which were of national interest and generally known, would be indifferent to the princesses. (Vol. i, p. 331.)

"Mr. Baird of Auchmedden in Aberdeenshire, has in one piece three young ladies, cousins, of the houses of Argyle, Errol and Kinnoul: Their ages, six, seven and eight, as marked on the side of the picture." It seems that this picture has no date; it was painted by George Jamesone (1586–1644), an early Scottish painter. (Vol. i, p. 349.)

An assembled family portrait of "Dr. Hibbard, physician, his wife, and five children. . . . Two children on the right hand were certainly added afterwards, and are much inferior to the rest. The dates were probably inserted at the same time." This portrait is by the well-known William Dobson. The description of it is quite indefinite, but if the picture is dated, and the ages of the several children added, it is an instance of the inclination in portraits of assembled families, to state the age of every member, girls as well as boys, without regard to the later inconvenience. (Vol. ii, p. 353.)

"At Wadham College, Oxford, is an excellent portrait of an old female servant of the College, inscribed: 'Mary George, Aetatis 120. Gul. Sonmans pinxit et dedit.'" (*Cf.* vol. iii, p. 973, note.) This is not dated. If Sonmans, or Sunman, came to England in the reign of Charles II, as is here said, this is one of the latest instances of this habit of inscribing on portraits the age of the person represented, here with more reason than usual. Another instance will be found, of the year 1667, at page 478. There is one of 1663 among the instances cited from the Louvre gallery. (Vol. ii, p. 520.)

In a list of the prints by Simon de Passe, an engraver of the time of James I, occurs this instance: "Matoaca, alias Rebecca, filia potentiss. princ. Powkatavi imp. Virginiae, aet. 21, 1616," the wife of John Rolfe. This Indian princess is more widely known as Pocahontas; as she was married, the inscription of her age was according to the rule as practised. (Vol. iii, p. 866.)

"Treasures of Art in Great Britain," by Dr. Waagen

Gallery of the Marquis of Hertford. Portraits of Philip Le Roy, Seigneur of Ravels, and of his lady, by A. Van Dyck. Inscriptions: On the portrait of the husband, "A. van Dyck, aetatis suae 34, Ao. 1630": On the portrait of his wife, "Aetatis suae 16. 1631." The convention was not extended to married ladies. (Vol. ii, p. 158.)

Sir Charles Eastlake's gallery. Portrait of an old lady, aged 83, by Rembrandt. This picture is now in the National Gallery and is mentioned under that heading. (Vol. ii, p. 264.)

Hampton Court. A portrait said to be of the father and mother of the younger Holbein, inscribed with the years of their age, 52 and 35 respectively, and the date of the painting, 1512. This portrait seems to be accepted by Mr. Wornum, in his study of Holbein, as having been painted by him at an early age, and may be taken to represent

married people. It is one of the earliest instances
of inscription-writing, and the portrait was
painted before Holbein came to England. (Vol.
ii, p. 362.)

Nostell Priory. The assembled family of Sir Thomas
More, after Holbein. This is one of the several
variant copies or completions of Holbein's lost
family portrait. The ages of the various members
of the family are inscribed on the picture; the
ladies of the family are all either married or betrothed; two or three servants of the household
also appear, but their ages are not given in the
copy, though one of them appears in the painter's
original sketch of the picture, where the age of
that person is given.

INSTANCES FROM CATALOGUES

The National Gallery (London)

Paris Bordone. Vol. i, p. 56. Portrait of a lady. Inscription: "Aetatis suae Ano. XVIII. Paris,
B. O." The portrait is not dated.

Rembrandt van Rijn. Vol. ii, p. 124. Portrait of a
lady, with white cap and ruff. Inscription: "Ae
sue 83. Rembrandt ft. 1634." The lady's age
takes her out of the conventional rule.

The National Portrait Gallery

School of Holbein. Vol. i, p. 25. Portrait of Queen
Catherine Howard. Inscription: "Aetatis suae
21." An inscription, but illegible in the reproduc-

tion, appears on the adjoining portrait of Queen Anne Boleyn.

Johannes Corvus. Vol. i, p. 30. Portrait of the Princess Mary Tudor, before her accession to the throne. Inscription: "Anno Dni 1544. Ladi Mari, doughter to the most vertuous prince King Henri the Eight. The age of XXVIII yeres." National interest in the three ladies last mentioned sufficiently explains the inscriptions; portraits of royal personages were perhaps particularly subject to posthumous labels. As the catalogue is made up of illustrations of the portraits, with only a slight description of them, the inscriptions must be gathered from the plates, but there do not seem to be any even remotely relevant to the double portrait, other than those here cited, and a miniature of Queen Elizabeth elsewhere described.

The Burlington Fine Arts Club. Early English Portraiture

Unidentified painter. Page 81. Portrait of an unknown lady, described thus: "Half length, three-quarters to right, fair hair parted in the middle and turned forward over the ears; black French hood; black dress lined with white fur, the sleeves puffed and slashed; both hands, folded before, hold a small book." Inscription: "Ano Dni 1551. Aetatis 34." It is said that the lady may have been a member of the Grey family. The painter's initials, H. E., may, it is said, possibly represent the painter, Haunce Eworth. In the absence of the portrait, which appears to be in the collection of the Duke of Norfolk, and of which there is no reproduction in the catalogue, it is difficult to learn what was the lady's appearance, but her age, and the use of the inscription, lead to an inference that the portrait, when examined, will rather resemble that of a matron. This portrait and a few others which are doubtful will be especially referred to again later on.

· Unknown painter. Page 101. Portrait of Margaret Wyat, Lady Lee (?) wife of Sir Anthony Lee (?). Inscription: "Etatis suae 34." This has no date; the reproduced portrait is distinctly like that of a matron.

Musée du Louvre. (*Fr. Villot*)

Philippe de Champaigne. Écoles Allemande, Flamande et Hollandaise, page 46. "Portrait d'une petite fille." Inscription: "Age 5 Ans 3 mois." This is not dated, and, at the child's age, would not in any event come under the rule, as it was practised.

Gerard Dou. Page 62. Portrait of an invalid lady, "La femme hydropique," and her daughter, a serving maid and a doctor. Inscription: "1663. G. Dov. oud. 65 jaer." The lady, as both aged and married, does not come within the rule.

Michiel-Jansz Mierevelt. Page 174. Portrait of a lady. Her description may be translated thus: The lady appears in three-quarter face to the left, wears a white cap (bonnet), adorned with lace (guipure), and a wide honeycomb ruff (fraise tuyautée), and has a golden chain about her neck. Her dress is black, the bodice ornamented with small studs (boutons); the cuffs or sleeve-facings (hautes manchettes) are long and ornamented with lace, and she holds in her left hand gloves embroidered with strawberries, birds and butterflies. Inscription: "Aetatis su. 34. Anno 1634." There is nothing known of this lady, and her circumstances in respect to marriage are unascertainable. The portrait may be classed with that of one of the ladies of like age, the lady, perhaps of the Grey family, mentioned in the Burlington catalogue (*supra*), and will be reviewed with it and some others later on.

Königliche Museen, Berlin

Antony Palamedes. Page 254. Portrait of a young girl. Inscription: "Ao. 16. A. Palamed." The portrait has no date.

Jacob Gerritz Cuyp. Page 254. Portrait of an old lady. Inscription: "Aetatis 68. Anno 1624. J. G. Cuyp fecit." The lady's age makes the rule inapplicable to her.

Michel Janze Mierevelt. Page 256. Portrait of an old lady. Inscription: "Ao. 1650. Aetatis 82." This instance is similar to the preceding.

Theodoor (Thomas?) de Keiser. Page 256. Portrait of an assembled and unidentified family. The picture shows a man, aged 48, seated at a table, his wife, aged 40, also seated, two sons, of 22 and 8 years standing, and three daughters of 19, 14 and 10 years respectively, also standing. The ages of the various persons are inscribed near them; the picture is not dated. It may be classed with the other pictures of assembled families, that of the Mytens family, noticed in the Dresden Gallery (*infra*), and with some other like instances mentioned hitherto. When such a portrait was also dated, the natural disinclination of the feminine members of the families to this procedure was overruled, evidently, by the general interest in the pictures as family records.

Belvedere-Galerie, Vienna

Andrea del Sarto. Italian Schools, vol. i, p. 294. Portrait of an old lady in a dark dress, seated with a book. Inscription: "An Aet. LXXII." The portrait is not dated.

Antonis Mor, known in England as Sir Anthony More. Schools of the Netherlands, vol. ii, p. 294. Portrait of an unknown lady. Her description may be translated as follows: A lady of rank, her left side turned toward the viewer, stands by a table on which she rests her right hand. She wears a dark velvet dress, with a long golden key-chain which she lifts with her left hand. Her hair, combed back, is covered with a lace cap. The open collar is bordered by a small ruff. On the shoulders the short sleeves are widely puffed; the close undersleeves, of a light material, end in ruffles at the wrists. Both hands are ornamented with rings. Dark background. Inscription: "1575. Aeta." The numerals signifying her age are missing, but the portrait itself, of which we have seen a reproduction, is of a typical matron of from forty to fifty years old.

Hans Burgkmair. German Schools, vol. iii, p. 41.
A portrait of himself and his wife by the painter.
Inscription: "Joann Burgkmair Maler LVII Alt.
Anna Allerlahn. Gemael. LII Jar Alt. MDXX-
VIIII. Mai. X. Tag." The Burgkmair and Holbein families were cotemporaries and closely
associated in Augsburg; the younger Holbein's
mother was, it is said, of the Burgkmair family
(*Holbein*, by R. N. Wornum, pp. 50, 57, 80); and
it was at Augsburg, probably, that he commenced
to place inscriptions on portraits, this fashion
having just arisen.

Unknown German painter. Vol. iii, p. 74. The description rendered into English, seems to be: A
lady of rank, thirty-one years old, stands in three-
quarter face, the left side toward the observer,
with her clasped hands resting on her dress. She
wears a red coat or gown extending to the ground,
with broad sleeve-facings of green velvet, with
which the gown is also bordered. On her breast
appears gold brocade with a white inner garment
which is fastened at the neck and is adorned with
gold lace to which pearls are attached. A cap
richly embroidered with pearls covers her hair,
two dissimilar gold chains are about the neck,
and at the waist a long girdle-ornament of gold
pieces depends. The background shows a grey
stone portal, with the inscription: "An. A. Nato
XPO MDXXV. Aetatis XXXI," and above it
appears a quotation from the Psalmist: "Non
derelinqua me une deus meus ne discesseris a me.
Psal. XXXVIII." The picture seems a memorial
of some calamity, and the lady doubtless had a

special reason for the inscription (Ps. 38, v. 21).
This excepts it from the usual rule. The portrait
is life-size. Whether the lady was married is
unknown.

The younger Holbein. Vol. iii, p. 135. Portrait of an
unknown lady ("Bildniss einer Frau"). The
description may be thus rendered: The twenty-
eight year old lady, with round face and retroussé
nose, in three-quarter face, and with her left side
turned towards the observer, gazes directly before
her. Over a white linen cap, under which a lock
of blond·hair appears, she wears a kind of yellow-
ish-white cloth hood. A black bodice with a very
narrow fur border half covers the breast, above
which, to high on the throat, extends a thin white
material. On the shoulders lies a small white
wrap. On the green background is inscribed:
"Etatis suae 28; Anno 1534." As the lady is
described by the writer of the description as Frau,
not Fraülein, she appeared to him to perhaps
resemble a matron, doubtless aiding his judgment by her age, while the presence of the inscription inclines the balance of evidence in the
same direction. This inscription, with some
other uncertain inscriptions, will be reviewed together as a class later on. We have recently
seen a reproduction of this portrait, which is
more attractive than the description would
seem to indicate, and are inclined to think that
in this case the presence of the inscription and
the lady's age should, there being no other evidence but the interesting picture itself, control
the decision.

Königliche Gemälde-Galerie, Dresden

Unknown Dutch artist. Page 91. Portrait of an unknown lady in a white cap or hood. Inscription: "Aetatis 41; Ao. 1548." At this lady's age, her matrimonial status being wholly unknown, the inscription cannot be considered as precedent for the inscription on the double portrait.

Van Dyck. Page 106. Portrait of an old lady. Inscription: "Aetatis suae 60; Anno 1618." This may be a companion picture to one next to it in the catalogue, of an old man, and with the same inscription: "Aetatis Suae 60; Anno 1618." The inscription is irrelevant as evidence here.

Portrait, page 137, by?——Mytens, of David Mytens, his wife and their five children, dated 1624, and inscribed with the age of each person. The sex and ages of the children are not mentioned in the catalogue. If there are girls past infancy, the inscription was not suitable in respect to them. For some other instances of this tendency to state all the ages in the pictures of assembled families, see the portraits of the family of Sir Thomas More, and some further instances, in the preceding lists.

Alte Pinakothek, Munich

Hans Mülich. Page 67. Portrait of an unknown lady, dated 1542, and inscribed: "1540 zalt do wart ich 37 jar alt." The picture is a companion piece to a portrait of a man by the same artist, and dated 1540, inscribed: "Etatis sue XXXVIII." From a comparison of the ages of the persons represented in the two portraits, some relation, very possibly of marriage, seems to be probable.

Thomas de Keyser. Page 80. Triple portrait. A young business man renders his accounts to his master. A lady holding an eyeglass sits in an armchair. Signed, "T. Keyser, 1650." Inscribed, near the lady, "Aetat. 6 z," and, near one of the men, "Aetat. z 6." The lady's age is not stated, or perhaps is in a cipher. The mutual meaning of the inscriptions is obscure.

Gerard Douffet. Page 175. Companion portraits of a merchant and his wife, dated 1617, and the ages inscribed, that of the merchant, 51, and of his wife, 57. This is quite irrelevant.

"The Complete Work of Rembrandt"

Vol. ii, No. 89. Portrait of Cornelia Pronck. Inscription: "Rembrandt f. 1633. Aet. 33." A companion picture of the husband of this lady adjoins it, and the instance is therefore irrelevant.

Vol. ii, No. 106. Portrait of a woman of eighty-three. *Vide supra*, catalogue of the National Gallery, London.

Vol. ii, No. 115. Portrait of a young woman of eighteen. Inscription: "Ae. sue. 18. Rembrandt f. 1634." We have to say of this portrait that it is not our ideal of a young lady of eighteen. The history of the portrait is not now ascertainable, and there is nothing to show that the young woman was unmarried. The countenance is distinctly unattractive; the general preface to the volume, which is usually commendatory, comments upon it adversely. As the inscription would be exceptional for an unmarried girl, as the young woman does not appear in the portrait as the distinctive type of an unmarried lady, as she may have been married, and as this would be the solitary instance in Rembrandt's work of such an inscription on the portrait of a young and unmarried woman, it cannot be affirmed that this is an exception to the rule of courtesy. This portrait will be referred to later on with a few other uncertain instances.

Vol. iii, No. 224. An old lady in an armchair. Inscription: "Rembrandt fc. 1635, Aet. sue 70, 24." The meaning of "24" is not at all clear. The "monogram" of Cordegliaghi, '24,'ᴬ in an instance from Morelli's *Italian Painters*, seems to resemble it. The lady is, from her age, beyond the intention of the convention.

Vol. iv, No. 278. An old lady with her hands clasped. Inscription: "Rembrandt f. 1640. Aet. suae 87." This portrait cannot be considered within the convention.

Vol. vi, No. 454. Portrait of a lady seated in a chair and looking at a parrot. Inscription: "Catrina Hoogsaet, oud 50 jaer, Rembrandt, 1657." In the Introduction, this lady is said, we know not on what authority, to be an old spinster. If she should be considered unmarried, her age still places her beyond the meaning of the convention.

Vol. viii, No. 560. A woman holding a hymn-book. Inscription: "Rt Van Ryn, 1632. Aet. 39." As the lady's matrimonial situation is unknown, her age and the presence of the inscription lead us to

infer that she was married. This portrait is one
of the few doubtful instances to be summed up
later on.

Precise statistics of Rembrandt's practice in
respect to inscriptions may be taken from his
work, and are as follows: His pictures number
595, of which 133 are portraits of ladies. Of
these last, the complete inscription of both date of
painting and age of the subject is placed on 7, the
age alone of the lady is given on none, the date of
painting alone is given on 74, and on 52 there is
no inscription; we pay no attention to the presence or absence of the signature of the artist, as
it has no bearing upon the matter before us. An
Appendix to the Edition, giving 21 lost and additional pictures known only through engravings,
does not give the inscriptions on the originals,
. and therefore is wholly omitted from our analysis.
Among the 133 portraits of ladies, if we try to
select from them the portraits of ladies who in
our best judgment are more probably young and
marriageable—though we have generally no
information as to whether they were or were not
married, and no definable rule at all to go by in
selecting them—we may perhaps select 41, of
which there are none whose inscriptions give the
lady's age only, 19 whose inscriptions give the
date of the portrait only, and 21 which bear no
inscription. There is but one of the 41, that of the
lady aged 18 and mentioned in the above list,
which has the inscription of age, and that portrait has the full inscription of both date and age,
and thus proves to be exceptional in its inscription

9

as it seems to be throughout. The remainder of the 133 portraits of ladies are either portraits of older ladies or of ladies known to be married, or otherwise unavailable. The tendency in Rembrandt's portraits of ladies is not, therefore, toward giving their ages. The only instances out of 133 portraits of ladies in which he did give them are the seven described at length in the above list, and he probably had special reasons in each of these cases for so doing.

Metropolitan Museum, N. Y., Loan Exhibition

Frans Hals. Portrait of Vrouw Bodolphe. Inscription: "Aetat. suae 73. Ano 1643. F. H." This lady was probably the wife of Heer Bodolphe, whose portrait, also by Frans Hals, adjoins this and has the same inscription, they being of the same age. (Page 134.)

Frans Hals. Portrait of Dorothea Berck. Inscription: "Aetat. suae 51. Ano 1644. F. H." The lady is said to have been the wife of the much younger man whose portrait adjoins hers. (Page 140.)

Neither of these portraits is relevant to the double portrait.

As many of the books and catalogues above listed contained no inscriptions which were precedents for, or conveyed any necessary information relative to that on the double portrait, they were not again referred to, though inscriptions occur in

all of them. In the instances cited, the evidence
which does not affirmatively sustain the position
taken in this Note, as to the inscriptions upon the
portraits of young and unmarried ladies, can be
called generally accidental rather than intentional,
and is not more than should be expected in a subject of this kind. The instances gathered from the
books in the preceding lists are much diversified,
and the reader might expect that there would inevitably be something among them which would
militate against the rule, but he will find on examination that there is no portrait which certainly
opposes it, and that, while there are a few uncertain instances, they are not numerous enough to
have importance as opposing evidence. These
doubtful inscriptions have been already commented upon in passing through the lists, but
we will assemble them for examination together
They are upon portraits of ladies of marriageable
age, but of whose circumstances, whether matrons
and permitting the inscription, or young and unmarried ladies and not permitting it, nothing further is known, namely: The portrait of a lady,
in the Burlington catalogue, perhaps of the Grey
family, aged thirty-four, a lady, in the Louvre
gallery, aged thirty-four, the lady in the Belvedere
gallery, Vienna, aged twenty-eight, Rembrandt's

ambiguous portrait of a young woman aged eighteen, and perhaps his portrait of a lady holding
a hymn-book, aged thirty-nine; the last two instances appear in the preceding list from Dr. Bode's
complete edition of Rembrandt. These cases are
essentially uncertain, but, as they are so remarkably few in number, it is much more probable that
they conformed to the general tendency, observ-
able in the practice of artists, to exclude such
inscriptions from the portraits of young and unmarried ladies, than that they were exceptions to
it. The objection, that is, that these cases might
be possibly exceptions to the practice, is less
probable than it is to suppose the practice to have
been generally recognized in these cases also, and
the ladies to have been matrons, there being no
other evidence as to the fact. In the case of the
lady aged eighteen, the evidence of the picture itself, which is reproduced by Dr. Bode, tends, when
supported by the uncertainty as to the lady's
marriage, and by the singularity of the inscription
in Rembrandt's work, to show that this was not a
genuine exception to the rule. A distinguishable
group of portraits, though hardly needing recapitu-
lation, is made by those of the More, Brooke,
Hibbard, one unnamed, and Mytens families of
children, with their parents, where the customary

courtesy was evidently disregarded in the desire to make a complete register of the assembled family. A third class of exceptional portraits, those of ladies who were also royal personages, has been repeatedly explained. The easel portraits assembled in the lists, and they are all that were observed as needing mention in the books and catalogues cited, will be found to give, in no instance, a clear precedent for the inscription on the double portrait.

We have, to speak figuratively, cast a net over these books and catalogues, both of miniatures and of easel portraits, and the returns, in the shape of inscriptions of the sort to which that on the double portrait belongs, have been very scanty. Considering that painters were, then, as they are now, at liberty to write their inscriptions as their discretion, or the interest of their employers, guided them, the paucity of the returns is certainly striking. It may be said that among all the instances collected in this essay, the only certain and complete precedent for, or rather example of, the inscription on the double portrait, is on a miniature, that of Mistress Holland, which, as it happened, was replaced by the lady in the next year. Surprising as it may be to believers in the enormous progress of our time over what has been before, the fact remains that the wishes of young women, in the Sixteenth and Seventeenth centuries, were regarded by painters in this matter, as is indicated by the all but non-appearance in the record examined of any portrait or miniature definitely infringing the rule. It was an unwritten law, the law of young women's wishes. The ages of all classes of people were described on their portraits by painters with the utmost freedom, but as to young girls they recognized a difference. In the full tide of inscription-writing on portraits, the convention of reserve as to the ages of young ladies was generally respected, the evidence of the family portraits examined placing the point beyond a reasonable doubt, unless further and opposing evidence can be found, which, in any considerable or noticeable amount, will not, as we think, probably be discovered.

The seven uncertain miniatures, which we left with a decision upon them in suspense, until an examination of the record of the easel portraits should show more fully what was the tendency of artists in this direction, if they are tested by the general tendency of painters, which is certainly sufficiently apparent in the larger portraits, must be allowed to have been probably the miniatures of married ladies, or else to have been unusual exceptions to a considerate and proper practice.

It can scarcely be doubted that the painter of the double portrait, if he added the inscription, went beyond the custom of artists, and took upon himself to place upon the portrait an inscription which was altogether unusual. As the reader has noticed, the collections consulted are only representative of the galleries, large and small, and the evidence is not perfect, as no examination could be exhaustive, and none such has been attempted. Other collections may contain instances of difficulty, but unless they should prove unexpectedly numerous and important, they could not justify a denial of the existence and recognition then, in the Sixteenth and Seventeenth centuries, of the natural reserve which has been referred to. The reader will find it possible with merely the evidence produced, we think, to decide as to this aspect of the Arbury portraits, the disregard in the double portrait of the usual courtesy to young ladies, and as to the inference, therefore, that the inscription was not cotemporary with but subsequent to the portrait. It should be said in passing that this argument is not without precedents; one will be found in Morelli's *Italian Painters*, above cited (vol. ii, p. 40), where there is a discussion whether an inscription on a painting of the Madonna by Palma Vecchio is cotemporaneous with the painting or a later addition, and this is held to affect Palma's position in history; the date of an inscription has not unfrequently been questioned.

As we have not seen the other older portraits at Arbury, even in photogravure, and know of their Latin labels only from Mr. Bridgeman's Appendix to Lady Newdegate's book, we are quite in the dark as to the precise lettering of those inscriptions, though it is understood that on several of those pictures the ages of the subjects of the portraits, and usually with them the dates of painting, are represented, nor do we know how many portraits are so marked, nor what are their dates and general appearance, nor whether they are of men or of women, nor whether the artists were of foreign or of native origin, but it is not expected that evidence from them will materially affect the evidence given by the double portrait, nor that as to its inscription. It is possible that in one or more of the older portraits, and not in a miniature, may be found the model from which the inscription on the double portrait was taken, and identification of it would perhaps be practicable and certainly interesting; an identification of it might be made, possibly, through the spelling.

The inscription which would be unconventional when the picture was painted would be natural and proper a century later. If Mary Fytton was the "Dark Lady," and the evidence that she was comes to the verge of proof, it is certainly obvious that the Latin inscription on the double portrait can not have been placed on it when the portrait was painted, as the portrait, necessarily in that case, would not contain her likeness. An older portrait was taken, probably, as a model in selecting the critical inscription at Arbury, but the evidence which can be found in the picture itself and in the inscription, the inconsistent minor details of the portrait, and the inconsistency with the inscription both of the evident age of the lady on the right in the portrait, and of the actual age of her supposed original, Mary Fytton, and the improbability that the artist would make publicly calculable the ages of the two young girls, leads to the belief that this happened, not when the portrait was painted, but long after the two young ladies were represented together in the double picture.

Leaving the inscription, we return to the portrait itself. The second portrait given to us in the Fytton Letters is like a replica in Court dress of the lady on the right in the double portrait, and has the same original. Some difference can certainly be found in the ages of the two faces, but it is not

enough to be at all material. The character of the
face of the lady upon the right in the double portrait is anything but that which we associate with
the rash and passionate type to which Mary Fytton belonged, and her distinct air of high reserve
is accentuated in the second, or Court, picture.
This difficulty has been felt by Lady Newdegate,
who expresses very clearly and frankly a doubt of
her position, by saying as to this second picture:

The expression has changed, under the schooling of
a Court life, to one of almost studied demureness, leading one to suspect a vein of subtlety beneath; or is it
because we know her history that we discern so much?
Gossip from a Muniment Room, 2d ed., p. 27.

The doubt as to this lady's expression and character which has been felt by Lady Newdegate will
be felt by nearly all other persons who study the
pictures. The inclination to regard her picture as
important in Shakspearean evidences has influ-
enced Lady Newdegate, and, besides, she could
support her identification of the portrait by a
study, perhaps not sufficiently thorough, of the
inscription. It is worth mention as to this second
portrait that Mr. Bridgeman admits (p. 173), "the
striking resemblance, especially about the mouth
and chin, to the younger girl in the double por-

trait." These two portraits at Arbury are not, however, the only representations of Mary Fytton. Far different are the challenging, provoking face and form, which are undoubtedly a representation of Mary Fytton, of the statue in the church at Gawsworth. It is, as it kneels there today, a pathetic figure, with a slightly mutinous expression, and assuredly with the face of a woman of quick wit. The countenance in the Arbury portraits seems, in comparison, order-loving, conventional, regulated, and wholly different in type, or so, at least, it has appeared to the writer of these pages. The statue is one of a group in a sepulchral monument on the north side of the chancel in the church of St. James. This church was formerly, in Mary Fytton's lifetime, splendidly and elaborately decorated, inside and out, with the shields of arms and, in the stained glass windows, the kneeling figures, of many generations of Fyttons and others. (Earwaker's *East Cheshire*, vol., ii, p. 575.) It is noteworthy that the effigy of Mary Fytton bears a marked family resemblance to that of her sister beside her, which the lady on the right in the double portrait does not bear to the lady painted with her. The statue of Anne resembles her portraits; the statue of Mary does not resemble the portraits attributed to her. Lady Newdegate, also, speaks of the lady in the second, or Court, portrait as giving the impression of a "tall, slight figure" (*Gossip from a Muniment Room*, 1st ed., p. 25), and this is true, but the statue of Mary at Gawsworth is not of that kind, but is of a decided figure of moderate height, and, indeed, does in no respect resemble the lady in the portraits. The thinness of figure is also noticeable in the lady on the right in the double portrait. The evidence of the statue is wholly contrary to the identification of her in the portraits at Arbury.

The two portraits at Arbury present the only difficult objection, to the theory, so far as we have noticed, that Mary Fytton was the original of the "Dark Lady." The evidence in support of that position, however, especially the statue at Gawsworth, is too strong and cumulative to be cancelled by family portraits which are, as a whole, of a very uncertain history. As it is said by Lady Newdegate, the correspondence as to Mary Fytton was kept locked up, even from the immediate family, for nearly three hundred years. What is more natural than that, through changes of ownership, and the very usual family forgetfulness, knowledge of the portrait should have become inaccurate, and that it should have been attributed to Mary Fytton because of its appearance in connection and on the same panel with that of the elder sister? When the portrait was seventy-five or a hundred years old the legend of Mary Fytton might easily lead to an attribution of it to her. In an article in *The Theatre* for December, 1897, the late Dr. F. J. Furnivall refers to Lady Newdegate's generous contribution to our knowledge of Mary Fytton, and alludes to still another portrait at Arbury, which is incorrectly labelled, as follows:

She has not given a photogravure of the third portrait, on wood, at Arbury, with the inscription:"Countess of Stamford, 2nd daughter of Sir Edward Fitton, Knt.," which she showed Mr. Tyler and me, in 1891, as one of Mary Fitton, and which is like enough to the other two portraits of Mary to be one of the same person, though it no doubt is that of Miss Mildred Maxey, who sent it to the first Lady Anne Newdigate [Mary's sister] at Arbury:

"I have, sweete sister lefte my pecter at my brother's loging for you. I think it not worth the trobbel in having it com downe, for it should have bine drane in a canfis [canvas], and this is a borde [board, panel]; but if my brother Cooke had bine in the tone [town], I wold [have] taken order with him for it; but I know if you do send to him, he will send it you in a case."

If Lady Newdegate, Mr. Tyler and I were right in accepting this portrait as Mary Fitton's in 1891, and Lady N. is right in changing her mind and saying now that it is Mildred Maxey's, may we not believe that all three portraits are those of Miss Maxey? Mr. Tyler has no doubt that they are. The Mildred portrait is certainly like, though not quite the same as, those claimed as Mary Fitton's: it is of a fair, red-and-white girl, with brown hair like Mary's and, too, with her dark, blue-grey eyes. Moreover, the hair of Mary's statue in Gawsworth Church seems once to have been coloured black; the colour can only be seen now in the interstices of the coils of hair, but assuredly it looks black. One cannot accept as conclusive the evidence of the Arbury portraits supposed to be those of Mary Fitton.

Dr. Furnivall meant to say Miss Cooke, not Miss Maxey. "Mildred (Cooke) Lady Maxey," as Lady Newdegate describes her for us, was own cousin to Sir Robert Cecil, the celebrated Secretary of State, whose mother was Lady Burghley, also Mildred, "the Lady Mildreda," daughter of the scholarly Sir Anthony Cooke, of Gidea Hall, Essex. The quotation illustrates in an amusing way the uncertainty which surrounds the pictures at Arbury, and how little reliance can be placed upon them as historical evidence. The unreliable Eighteenth century inscription again connects the third picture with Mary Fytton by calling it "2nd daughter of Sir Edward Fitton, Knt.," but also calling it, "Countess of Stamford."

Mr. Bridgeman observes that at Arbury, Anne "would be within a drive of Hartshill, near Atherstone, then the residence of Mildred's father,

William Cooke, second son of Sir Anthony Cooke."
Atherstone lies 5½ miles N. N. W. from Arbury
Hall, on a fairly direct road, Hartshill being between the two, and three miles distant from Arbury
Hall, according to the English Ordnance Map, if
the roads then were as those of today. Mr. Bridgeman further says of this (p. 170): "I may observe
in passing that I can find no evidence that Lady
Newdigate was even acquainted with Mildred
Cooke till after 1596, about which year the former
came to live at Arbury."   Mr. Bridgeman does not
remember that Anne's was a childhood marriage,
and occurred when she was twelve years old, in
1587 (p. 3), the year after that in which Arbury
was purchased by the Newdigate family (p. 2).
This is some evidence, stronger or weaker, but still
evidence, that Anne was acquainted with her
young husband's neighbours, in whom she had an
approaching though still future interest, for surely
some of them might visit her. The evidence, such
as it is, is in plain view. Mr. Bridgeman further
says (p. 172), that Lady Maxey and also Lady
Grey were "on terms of intimacy with Lady
Newdigate," and among the number of ladies who
familiarly addressed her in their correspondence as
"sister." He inclines, however (p. 173), to accept
the third picture as one of Lady Grey, on the basis

of the Eighteenth century inscription on the portrait, which, with the error usual in the Eighteenth century inscriptions, refers to the Grey-Stamford family, and he depends upon the mentioning of a portrait of that lady in Lady Newdigate's Will. But Miss Mildred's letter certainly shows that a portrait of her was to be sent to Arbury, and without considering the degree of resemblance which the third portrait is said to bear to the double portrait and the second portrait, we can at the least say that there is no preponderant evidence as to it in either the one direction or in the other.

An aunt of Mildred Cooke, also Mildred Cooke, was the wife of the Lord High Treasurer, the illustrious Lord Burghley, and the mother of Sir Robert Cecil; another aunt, Anne Cooke, was the wife of the Lord Keeper of the Great Seal, Sir Nicholas Bacon, and mother of Anthony and Francis Bacon. As Mildred Cooke was so highly connected, it is by no means improbable that she should have been the lady in the second portrait, the lady in the magnificent Court dress. She would, then, be the lady painted with Anne in the double portrait. This is nothing but a surmise, but it accords with the portrait both in this respect and in her age, nineteen, and also in her situation as a very near neighbour of Anne's in the latter's future home at Arbury.

It is a question for students of the portraits of Queen Elizabeth's days, whether her face, in its expression of reserved intellectuality, has not a certain degree of family resemblance to that of Sir Robert Cecil. Certainly it is not in the least like that of Anne Fytton, either in the double portrait or in that lady's other likenesses, and it is assuredly in the second portrait, that of a lady of great distinction. A comparison with the features of her aunt, Lady Burghley, and of Sir Robert Cecil, her cousin, however, does not show any marked resemblance, the long, pointed chin and compressed lips characteristic of them not being distinctly marked in Mildred's face; she still may have resembled her mother's family in this. Lady Burghley's portrait gives the impression of a tall, slight figure such as Mildred's, that is, such as the figure of the lady in the second portrait.

The holly and the palm, devices, either badges or charges, sketched on the sleeves of the lady on the right in the double portrait, it seems not possible now to connect with Mildred Cooke's family in any of its known branches, nor has any evidence been found through these emblems identifying the lady on the right in any particular. The quarterings of Miss Mildred's aunt and namesake, Lady Burghley's, shield of arms are said to be: 1. Cooke;

2. Malpas; 3. Machyn; 4. Belknap; 5. Boteler; 6. Sudeley; 7. Mountford; (*Historical Monograph, William Cecil, Lord Burghley*, by the Rev'd Augustus Jessop and others, with portraits of the Cecils, p. 98), but whether any of these families or others in the ancestry of Anne Fytton's friend and future neighbour, Miss Mildred, used the palm or holly as either a badge or charge is an elusive question. They do not appear as charges in the blazoning of the arms of these families in Burke's *Armorial Bearings*, but they might be badges, and therefore less formal and more easily transmissible. Though Mildred Cooke's mother, if an heiress, could transmit them as armorial bearings, and could indifferently transmit them as badges, supposing her to have a right, her name and family are not stated in any book examined by us. The palm and holly have been used quite frequently in heraldry; we have gathered a little unconnected and apparently unconnectable evidence as to them. A John le Bouteller is mentioned among the Normans in the first Crusade on a roll in the Library of Bayeux Cathedral. There were several families of this or of a derivative name in England, among them the one quartered in Lady Burghley's shield. A Ralph Boteler appears among the Crusaders in the second Crusade (*The English Crusaders*, by

J. C. Dansey, London, 1849,?). Their descendants, some of them, might perhaps use the palm as a badge. The palm several times occurs on escutcheons or crests. A Christopher Cooke of Alresford, Hants, in the last century, had, as a part of his crest, a wreath, not of holly but of laurel, a different leaf. (William Berry, *Encyclopaedia Heraldica*, vol. ii, London, 1828.) The evidence is scanty, nothing. But it has not been suggested by Mr. Bridgeman or by Lady Newdegate, who have access to some at least of the family records, that these emblems were ever used by the Fyttons indeed, they say little of them; their presence on the dress of the lady on the right in the double portrait makes it particularly improbable to claim her as a daughter of the Fyttons, and especially as a younger daughter. The question is yet open for elucidation, and the decisive evidence of the palm and holly must be left here uninterpreted.

A list of Lady Anne Newdigate's feminine correspondents and friends would be of advantage in this search, and might perhaps be given to the public. Two other of her most intimate friends; who might perhaps have been represented in the double portrait, and not Mistress Mildred Cooke, are, first, Elizabeth, daughter of Edward Neville,

Lord Abergavenny, and wife of Sir John Grey, of Groby. Groby is in Leicestershire, 4½ miles from Leicester, and distant, in a direct line, sixteen miles northeast from Arbury. "The Manor was the birthplace of Lady Jane Grey (1537–1554), who was Queen of England for thirteen days." (*Bartholomew's Gazetteer*, 1893.) The other of the two ladies was also Elizabeth, and was the wife of Sir John Ashburnham and daughter of Sir Thomas Beaumont. Sir Thomas, who married an heiress, had two residences, one at Stoughton Grange, Leicestershire, and the other, where he resided at times, at Bedworth, which lies two miles southeast from Arbury, two and a half miles by road. Anne is mentioned in her correspondence as visiting there, and seems to have been on most friendly terms with the family. At least seven families have at some time borne holly leaves on their escutcheons, but to connect them with the friends of Anne Fytton requires fortunate research, viz., Worthington, Woodward, Weston, Aernest, Hussey, Hollingworth, and Moody or Mody. (Glover's Ordinary of Arms, Appendix to Edmondson, vol. i; Aubrey's *Wiltshire*, Part 1, p. 25.) Badges were usually painted or embroidered on banners, liveries of soldiers, followers and retainers, etc.; they were distinct from and independent of the coat armour. Badges were greatly in vogue in England from the reign of King Edward I until that of Queen Elizabeth, when they fell into disuse. (J. Edmondson, *A Complete Body of Heraldry*, vol. i, p. 189, London, 1780.) The holly was the badge of Clan Drummond, we are told. The Scottish coat of Irvine of Drum bears holly leaves. (J. Woodward, *Treatise on Heraldry*, vol. i, p. 337.) The evidence amounts to nothing. An inquiry at the College of Arms, London, as to Miss Mildred Cooke, Lady Grey and Lady Ashburnham, has had the following courteous answer:

The mother of Mildred Cooke was Frances Grey, daughter of John Grey, brother of the Duke of Suffolk. I do not think either holly or palm fit in with this Mildred. Her descent was roughly as follows: I. Philip Cooke, married Elizabeth, daughter and heiress of Sir Henry Belknape. II. Sir John Cooke, married Alice, daughter and heiress of Sir William Saunders of Banbury. III. Sir Anthony Cooke, married Anne Fitz-William. IV. William Cooke, married Frances Grey. V. Mildred Cooke. It is difficult to speak with certainty about badges. Not all families bore them, nor is it certain that all are recorded as in the case of Arms, though many are. The arms and crest of the Maxeys were talbots' heads. I know of no badge. The Greys, of course, did not bear either holly or palm. The Fitz-Williams bore a trefoil as a badge. It could hardly be mistaken for holly, I should think. The Saunders bore elephants' heads in their arms and crest. The Belknapes bore a lizard as a badge. I cannot see how either holly or palm could come in here.

Elizabeth, daughter of Sir Thomas Beaumont, and wife of Sir John Ashburnham, seems to me to present more possibilities. The crest of the Ashburnhams was an ash tree out of a coronet, and the Beaumonts are said to have born a badge of a broom cod (though I cannot trace here any definite authority for it). The broom cod has somewhat the semblance of palm, and if the holly might, perchance, be ash, the identification seems possible, though I think it must be taken with reserve. The Beaumonts had a Plantagenet descent, which may have accounted for their use of the broom, if a fact. I cannot find any record of either holly or palm used as a badge at that period, nor can I trace the descent of any of the three ladies you name, so far as I have been able to find them from our records, to any family who bore either holly or palm in their arms, certainly as regards direct descent; of course the female descent of every family spreads indefinitely, and it would be impossible even in a lifetime to trace all the ramifications of all the females. But taking the more immediate descent, and the probability that the badges (if they be such), refer to the male descent, or at most to an immediate female ancestor, I think the suggestion I have given affords the only possible clue out of the three ladies whose names you give me to work on; but I repeat that you cannot regard the matter as absolutely proved, even if the badges, when examined, can be read into the proposed form. It cannot be put higher than conjecture, with a reasonable possibility, taking into consideration all the circumstances.

Mr. Bridgeman observes that Mildred (Cooke), Lady Maxey, could not have been painted on the double portrait because she "was baptized at Romford in September, 1573, so that in 1592 [the date painted on the double portrait] she would have been in her nineteenth not her fifteenth year," thus not according with the age, fifteen, given to the subject of the portrait by the inscription, but if the maker of the inscription thought that her portrait was that of Mary Fytton the argument is beside the question. Her greater age than Anne's accords with the appearance of the faces of the two ladies in the double portrait. Mr. Bridgeman makes a point of the "*a priori* probability" that if two girls are painted together they are related; a probability, it is conceded, but not a certainty. Two young women, if intimate friends, might be represented in a picture together. If Mildred Cooke, Anne's future neighbour, or any other intimate friend, was visiting Anne at Gawsworth, Anne might think it proper to be represented in a picture with her.

Lady Ashburnham and many other ladies addressed Anne as "Sister," as was the fashion of the time (*Gossip from a Muniment Room*, the Fytton Letters, 1st ed., pp. 50, 124, 135; *Meas. for Meas.*, I, iv, 47; *M. N. Dream*, III, ii, 199); another of her "intimate" friends was Margaret, Lady Hoby, daughter of Lord Hunsdon; she had a large acquaintance among her own sex, one among them of general interest being the unfortunate Lady Arabella Stuart, of the blood royal, later a victim of State policy. The evidence inclines to the theory, furthermore, that she was one of the young ladies who are contented with and fond of their girl friends, as she did not leave her father's house for that of her young husband, to whom she had been married in childhood, until she was twenty-one or twenty-two years old. One of Anne's characteristics, therefore, seems to have been her disposition to friendships with other ladies, and this strengthens the probability that the lady painted in the portrait with her was one of her many friends instead of her sister, Mary Fytton. Moreover, Mary, in her girlhood, did not live at Arbury, in Warwickshire, whither her sister did not go until after the picture had been painted. Mary lived at her father's house, at Gawsworth, in Cheshire, and as the picture was doubtless taken by Anne to her husband's house, at Arbury, when she entered upon her married life there, no inference can be made from its appearing on the walls of Arbury to the effect that it is a portrait of Mary; if it was a portrait of one of Anne's girl friends, it would inevitably go with her to Arbury; as Mary did not live at Arbury but at Gawsworth, the absence of any portrait of her at Arbury does not call for an explanation. Looking at the particular circumstances of the case, if there had been ever any portraits of Mary Fytton, of the larger and ceremonial kind, at Arbury, they might and unquestionably would have been banished from the family gallery and put out of sight, and this would also make it rather more probable that the portraits which are there today, especially the second and single portrait in Court dress, are not of her. There is no compelling reason apparent for regarding the double portrait as a portrait of two sisters excepting the inscription alone, and when the very considerable evidence, both within and dehors the portrait, and opposing the inference that the inscription was cotemporary with the portrait, is considered, our conclusion as to the inscription appears to be not only sound, but to resemble also that reached as to the other elements of the portrait, the conclusion that the picture did not represent the two sisters, and besides, the evident disagreement between the inscription, which refers to the Fytton sisters, and the portrait, which does not bear the inscription out at all, shows of itself that the inscription was later than the portrait, and also mistaken as to one of the ladies represented.

Lady Anne Newdigate's bequest to one of her daughters, Lettice, of "my tablet with my sister picture in it," as the phrase appears in her Will, is, at the present time, indefinite in its description, but Mr. Bridgeman presses the point a little. As she speaks of "my" picture, she so distinguished it from the others which her late husband, Sir John, had doubtless made a disposition of by his Will, they ordinarily following the estate to the heir. It is very likely that the "tablet" in question was some combination, a fanciful article, akin to the "gownes, petticoats, jewells" and other valuables, possibly the paraphernalia, not mentioned for us in further detail in the quotation from the Will in the Fytton Letters, and which were divided among the five children, probably a miniature, and the subject of a special bequest. Various similar, indeed almost identical, instances of the use of the word "tablet" in connection with miniatures, will be found in the mention of the accounts of George Heriot (he is remembered in *The Fortunes of Nigel*), of Edinburgh, goldsmith to James I and his Queen, in the Morgan Catalogue of Miniatures, vol. i, p. 52. Lady Newdigate speaks as though there were but one object to which her words could be applied. A miniature of Queen Elizabeth is said to have been "mounted in a box." (Williamson's *History of Portrait Miniatures*, vol. i, p. 12.) Another of Sir Kenelm Digby and Lady Digby (1633), "is set in gold, richly inlaid with flowers in enamel, and shuts like a book." (*Ibid.*, p. 30.) It is certainly possible that the "tablet with my sister picture in it" was something of this kind. But it is plain that Lady Newdigate would not usually have a power of disposition over the easel portraits, and that the "tablet" therefore stood on a different footing from them, and was accurately described in the clause in her Will.

The bequest, then, was of a portrait of Mary, but not a part of the gallery at Arbury; this portrait, whose existence is known only through this reference to it in the Will, must have perished through neglect or indifference, or through accident, or have been lost to sight in some way, as otherwise it would have been a bar to the mistake made in later years in respect to Mary's likeness in the double portrait. The customary fate of old portraits is described by Dr. Propert, in his *History of Miniature Art*, p. 41, quoting Horace Walpole. Horace Walpole's paragraph on "the gradual decay and removal of family pictures" is a vivid one, and is especially applicable to portraits or miniatures which have no family value to recommend them. (*Anecdotes of Painting*, Wornum's ed., vol. ii, p. 656.) A miniature valued as little as Mary's was likely to be, after her sister's death, or a combination of portrait and "tablet," would have no kindly fate; it might have been taken back by Mary after Lettice' death in 1625, unmarried, and after Anne's death in 1618, and have disappeared or have been neglected or ruined in many ways.

Mr. Tyler's investigations have shown that the monumental effigies of the Fytton family, in Gawsworth Church, Cheshire, representing the Fytton family, among them Lady Fytton, seated and leaning her head on her hand, her daughter, Anne, and her second daughter, Mary Fytton, both kneeling, are statues coloured originally to resemble life, in which opinion Mr. Bridgeman seems to concur. Mr. Tyler declares that Mary Fytton's statue has, or had, black hair and eyes as has the lady of the sonnets. Mr. Bridgeman, who takes a different view, says: "I do not dispute the fact that, so far as any traces of colouring remain on the monument, Mary Fitton's hair and complexion appear to be distinctly darker than they are shown in the pictures," but he ascribes this colour to "the dust and grime of centuries," a statement which is positively traversed by Mr. Tyler, and in which he is to some extent, as we have seen, followed by Dr. Furnivall. The statue is, beyond doubt, authentic. The spectator clearly recognizes in this effigy the clever and forward type of lady to which Mary Fytton belonged; the statues, as they were coloured, were certainly intended, at least, to be semblances of the originals. The sculptor succeeded in his attempted semblance of Anne, as we can see by comparing that statue with her portraits.

The portraits called Mary Fytton's at Arbury, in Warwickshire, have blue-grey eyes and brown hair, and show that Mary Fytton was not the original of the "Dark Lady." But that they are likenesses of Mary Fytton is well contested by Mr. Tyler, and an attempt in the same direction is made in these pages. Her sister, Anne, in the double portrait, according to Lady Newdegate, "has dark hair and eyes and arched eyebrows." There are three other portraits, which appear to give the same record of her, at Arbury. The controversy appears in Lady Newdegate's *Gossip from a Muniment Room*, the Fytton Letters, 2d ed., London, 1898, with an Appendix by Mr. C. G. O. Bridgeman, and in Mr. Tyler's *The Herbert-Fytton Theory: a Reply*, London, 1898, with a photograph of the statues at Gawsworth, and in his edition of the sonnets. Plays upon Mary Fytton's story are: "Shakspeare and his Love," by Frank Harris, with an introduction (London, 1910); "The Dark Lady of the Sonnets," by G. Bernard Shaw, published in a book with "Misalliance" and "Fanny's First Play," and with observations upon the Arbury portraits (Brentano, New York, 1914); and "Mary, Mary," by George Gordon (C. C. Baldwin), in a book entitled *Airy Nothings, or What You Will* (New York, 1917).

If we were to indite a play on the subject of this Note, we might be led to introduce a scene in which the poet, on one of his visits to Warwickshire called on Mary at Arbury in 1602, a final visit,—in the absence of the Newdigates—and we would bring them before the double portrait, and saying of it:

S.   Who is that with your sister?

M.   That is a relative of the Cecils, Mildred Cooke, she was, a great friend of my sister's, married now.

S.   No doubt it is much valued by Mrs. Newdigate.

M.   Not for the artist.

S.   Who was he?

M.   Some one staying at Macclesfield, I think; I forget his name. They did it on impulse, but Anne thinks the world of it now.

S.   The world does not insure portraits that stay unlabelled.

M.   I believe there is a paper on its back with the names, but it must be ten years old now, and I do not know if the paper is there.

It is improbable that any such incident ever took place, and perhaps we violate the best canons of historical play-writing in suggesting it, but if it can bring before the reader more clearly our theories as to this portrait, and its origin, it will have fulfilled its purpose. Arbury, in the Eighteenth-Nineteenth Century, is described as "Cheverel Manor" in *Mr. Gilfil's Love Story;* Sir Roger Newdigate, the identifier of the portraits of 1768, is Sir Christopher Cheverel; the novelist was born on the estate.

MISCELLANEOUS POINTS

Mistress Mary Fytton seems, in 1598 or 1599, to have become, perhaps, one of the subscribers to an undertaking by one of the members of Shakspeare's Company to dance the Morris from London to Norwich; at all events, she was selected by him for the dedication of the book in which he recounted this memorable exploit. The book is William Kempe's *Nine daies Wonder, Performed in a daunce from London to Norwich* (London, 1600), dedicated:

To the True Ennobled Lady, and his most bountifull Mistris, Mistris Anne Fitton, Mayde of Honour to the most sacred Mayde, Royall Queene Elizabeth.

This is a merry book. Kempe is remembered in Shakspearean annals as, at that time, the Clown, jig-maker, and player of Low Comedy parts in the Lord Chamberlain's, that is, Shakspeare's Company. His book tells us: On "the first mundaye in Lent," 1599, I "began frolickly to foote it from the right honorable the Lord Mayor's of London towards the right Worshipfull (and truely bountifull) Master Mayor's of Norwich," covering the distance, about one hundred miles, in nine days, not continuously. The reader will be interested to know that his route lay through Romford, Chelmsford, Braintree, Sudbury, Bury St. Edmunds, Thetford and Hingham, and that he was attended sometimes by hundreds of people, some dancers among them volunteering to put on the bells as Morris dancers (*II Hen. VI*, III, i, 366), and join him in his very rapid forward dance to pipe and tabor. He describes the journey in ample

detail.   His "Epistle Dedicatorie" concludes as
follows:

But, in a word, your poore servant offers the truth
of his progresse and profit to your honorable view:
receive it, I beseech you, such as it is, rude and plaine,
for I know your pure judgement lookes as soone to see
beauty in a Blackamoore, or hear smooth speech from
a Stammerer, as to finde anything but blunt mirth
in a Morrice dauncer, especially such a one as
Will Kemp, that hath spent his life in mad Jigges and
merry jestes.   Three reasons moove mee to make pub-
lik this journey: one to reprove lying fooles I never
knew; the other to comend loving friends, which by
the way I daily found; the third to shew my duety to
your honorable selfe, whose favours (among other
bountifull friends) makes me (dispight of this sad
world) judge my hart Corke and my heeles feathers, so
that me thinkes I could flye to Rome (at least hop to
Rome, as the old Proverbe is) with a morter on my
head.   In which light conceite I lowly begge pardon
and leave, for my Tabrer strikes his huntsup, I must
to Norwich: Imagine, noble Mistris, I am now setting
from my Lord Mayor's, the houre about seaven, the
morning gloomy, the company many, my hart merry.
Your worthy Ladiships most
unworthy servant
WILLIAM KEMP.

As to the reference to a "Blackamoore," which
has been made a matter of question, a reference
which certainly should not occur in an address to

a brunette, or to a lady of so dark a complexion as
the identifiers of Mary Fytton with the "Dark
Lady" think her to have had, as Kempe stated her
name incorrectly in his dedication to her of the
book, seeming to have confounded her name with
that of her sister, of whom, also, he knew little,
as that lady was then married, and had changed
her family name, it may be properly inferred that
his knowledge of her was distant, and only that of
the generality of actors, and it is probable, therefore, that he never thought at all of her complexion,
when writing his book. While the names of ladies
of position are often discussed, their complexions
are far less heard of by the public. The book is
evidence that Mistress Fytton was a name particularly known to Shakspeare's Company, whether
through her portrayal as Rosaline, not long before,
in *Love's Labour's Lost*, or because of her rumoured
interest in their fellow-actor, Shakspeare, or
through her general prominence, or in some other
manner, the reader can consider from the evidence
we have as to her life. Her selection among the
other subscribers or contributors, or, if they are not
implied by his words, and they certainly seem to be
so, the selection of herself merely, to receive the
dedication, indicates a preference of her, and by a
member of Shakspeare's Company. If it were true

that there was that which made rumours of her
run through the membership of the Company, the
whispers of "lying fooles," after the publication of
The Passionate Pilgrim, for instance, in the year
before Kempe published his account of his trip,
Kempe's allusion—as it is hard to assign limits to
what so inveterate a jester might say—might be
merely his unrestrainable habit of speech put in
writing. But such an interpretation appears quite
unnecessary. The word "Blackamoore" is an
allusion used in the merry vein in which the book
is written, and therefore had no personal intention,
and his mistaking her baptismal name, and the
conventional style of his more direct address to
her, with his free manner of speech otherwise,
indicate that his knowledge of her was distant and
impersonal, and that he merely blundered in his
characteristically outspoken address. Blacka-
moors were still few in the days of Queen Elizabeth,
alluded to as evidences of the outlying world of dis-
covery and adventure, and this, of course, was the
motive for Kempe's careless reference to them.
Mary Fytton's sister was, as we know, Anne, but
not Anne Fitton, as she had been married long
before, by contract for thirteen, actually for about
four or five years, and at that time, of course, was
addressed by her husband's name, Newdigate, and

particularly in matters of form, such as this dedication; she was never a Maid of Honour, though from time to time she must have come to London, where her father had a house, and to the Court, and thus had been heard of by Kempe sufficiently to confuse her name with her sister's. She was assuredly of a dark complexion. The book, then, is evidence that Shakspeare's Company had heard of this Maid of Honour somewhat more than of the others, but very questionable evidence as to Mary's complexion. The book is clear evidence that Kempe had no personal acquaintance with her sister, Mrs. Newdigate, for when he alluded in his book to a Blackamoor, he could not have thought of her complexion. He might have known of Mary's complexion and not of her sister's, we admit, but it is no less true that his knowledge of neither was accurate in respect to their names. While it is plain that there was an innuendo in his words, the best inference from the book, and from what little we know of him, and of his and of most other common actors' probable relations with the Court, is that he was not thinking about the lady's complexion at all when he wrote them, and that the references to a Blackamoor and to a Stammerer were only the studied expression in his writing of the tested and proved witticisms with which he was wont to entertain his audiences, at times, in the theatres.

A sonnet suitable for private reading only, and whose existence is all but positive proof that this series of sonnets was never intended by Shakspeare for publication, has been, with some reason, said to bear upon the question at issue, whether the "Dark Lady" was Mary Fytton. Shakspeare speaks, in the intimate sonnet, CLI, of a "triumph of love," and of her as his "triumphant prize," which would agree with an intrigue with a personage of the Court, and it seems to be probable that he cites her name as if in fault, "thy name," *i. e.*, Fitton. Mr. Tyler has discussed this matter in his edition of the sonnets, pp. 82, 313, referring to *Cymbeline*, IV, i, 6. In Ormerod's *History of Cheshire* (2d ed., London, 1882, vol. iii, p. 550), in speaking of the ruins of the old Hall of the Fyttons at Gawsworth, the author says:

Over the door of the old hall is a carved representation of the coat of Fitton, with sixteen quarterings, with a motto in a garter introducing the words FIT ONUS LEVE in allusion to the name.

A Latin inscription under the sculpture records that it was made at Galway in Ireland, "Galviae in

Hibernia," in 1570 for Sir Edward Fyton, Lord President of the Council for Connaught and Thomond. He was also the "Treasurer at Wars, Vice-Treasurer and General Receiver" for Ireland, and he was paternal grandfather to Mary Fytton. Mr. J. A. Froude in his History of England (vol. x, p. 515), mentions him in a picturesque and characteristic circumstance. Sir Edward was one of the energetic and notable men of his day. There is a fine brass to him, mentioning also his wife and fifteen children, in St. Patrick's Cathedral in Dublin. (Ormerod, *loc. cit.;* Murray's *Handbook for Ireland.*) The allusion in the motto was perhaps to the duties of his office in Ireland, that is, that he was *fit* for them, and they a light burden, or, as a friend suggests, to whom the problem was put, that he was *fit* for his position, and his rule a light burden on Ireland. Literally it is: The burden is made light. Curious passages, playing on the word, occur in *Love's Labour's Lost*, IV, i, 131, 145, and see *Twelfth Night*, III, i, 21.

On the Fytton monument in the church at Gawsworth is a tablet with verses, concluding thus:

Here's the blest man, his wife the fruitfull vine,
The children th' olive plants, a gracefull line,
Whose soule's and body's virtues sentence them
FITTONS, to weare a heavenly diadem.

The punctuation and capitals are as given by Dr. Ormerod. The meaning of the last line is, of course, that the family were *fit ones* to wear the diadem. The reference is to the family of the first baronet, Sir Edward, Mary's brother, who had twelve children.

Perhaps the name Mary gave to her horse, "Grey Fitton," which was kept for her in 1598 at the Queen's stables, was another instance of this play upon the name. (Cal. Salis. MSS., Part 8, p. 417.) There seems to be no reason to doubt that the name was punned on at times, and perhaps habitually, by the family, which would explain Shakspeare's words, "thy name."

Sir Edward Fytton, the father of Mary Fytton and son of the Sir Edward Fytton first mentioned, was also greatly interested in Ireland as patentee of 11,515 acres in Munster (the reader will be interested to observe that there is a curious reference to Ireland, in connection with verse-writing to a lady, in *As You Like It*, III, ii, 187; Hamlet also, without necessity, invokes St. Patrick as witness to the trouble about him, I, v, 136), and he is said to have held office for some years as Lord President of Munster. (Earwaker's *East Cheshire*, vol. ii, p. 555.) He appears to have been a Member of Parliament; he was Mayor of Macclesfield in

Cheshire (1599–1602). Gawsworth, where was the family residence, is a village about three miles S. W. of Macclesfield. It is said, however, that he was disappointed in not succeeding his father as Vice-Treasurer of Ireland; he seems not to have been so stirring a man.

Sonnet CXLII criticises the lady of the sonnets, and perhaps refers in part to the circumstances upon which CLII, 1–4, is based. Line 8 of CXLII, if compared with his general portrait of the lady, and with CXL, 9–14, can best be taken with much reserve, and as pointing partly, perhaps, to the lady's indifferent treatment of her marriage engagements, and chiefly to her lover's family. The poet's disposition seems to have been toward jealous and severe utterances, as in CXXXVII, 6, which rather refers to a common inclination toward all men, or, more precisely, to his "over-partial looks" as having been placed in competition with those of others, than to anything more serious. The same undue reproach is found in his violent words in CXLVII, 14, in all probability not as yet quite justified, and in the jealous censures of CXXXI, 13, and CXLVIII, 14. From the point of view of an interpretation of the sonnets as if addressed to Mary Fytton, there is no doubt that the poet was too severe, but also that he had cause for his reproaches, for he was not the only one who questioned the lady's conduct, as we shall see further on.

In *The Passionate Pilgrim* (No. 1), occurs a variant or draught of CXXXVIII, containing the following quatrain:

But wherefore says my love that she is young?
And wherefore say not I that I am old?
O, love's best habit is a soothing tongue,
And age, in love, loves not to have years told.

The first line has been changed in the later version of the Quarto, as follows:

But wherefore says she not she is unjust?
And wherefore say not I that I am old?
O, love's best habit is in seeming trust,
And age, in love, loves not to have years told.

The phrase "that she is young," which has sometimes been thought to show that the "Dark Lady" was past her youth, can be understood when we remember that Mary Fytton became twenty years old in June, 1598, the year in which the sonnet was probably written, Shakspeare himself being at the time thirty-four, and the line therefore can be taken as a gentle reminder of the interesting cir-

cumstance. The lady's lack of explicitness in the
version in *The Passionate Pilgrim*, is as to her age;
in the version in the Quarto it is turned as to his
age exclusively, the original statement referring to
her age having been changed, it may be, because of
its publication in *The Passionate Pilgrim*, or, perhaps, independently of that publication, through
general principles of reserve. Lord Herbert probably came to Court in June, 1598, and therefore
about at the date of this sonnet, which was accordingly one of the earlier of the series, and unaffected
by his influence, as was CLI, and this is confirmed
by both its manner and its matter.

The sonnets to the "Dark Lady" are strange
sonnets for so great a man, but they will seem to be
so only until their author's mind, the direct habit
of speaking of the day, and the involved circumstances of the case, are taken into account. It is
most unlikely that they were published on his
initiative, or that they were circulated in MS. at
all. They are easy to censure, and yet there
breathes through them a spirit of self-reproach that
in part redeems them, and redeems their writer
from the imputation, if any should attempt to
bring it, of moral indifference. The moral struggle,
which is so plainly evident, raises them far above

the mere verses of animal passion of which there were many in the days of the English Renaissance, but from which class of writing they are widely separated. More and more enamoured, and unable for more than one reason to marry, he was for a time overborne by his passion, and these sonnets are a record of his romance and of his regret, a record of regret basing itself on facts, and coming, as we may think, in true Shakspearean manner, to an unshakable conclusion. No man who has studied the bright row of Shakspeare's heroines, from Juliet to Perdita, Miranda and Imogene, can understand him as other than a respecter of womanhood.

As to *Antony and Cleopatra*, if any one of his plays is his masterpiece, in respect to his general ability, it is this. The first scene, in which he moves with ease in a gigantic power, the passage where Cleopatra makes Antony a mock reverence —"I'll seem the fool I am not; Antony will be himself."—is written in a very great style; you cannot match it, in that respect, in *Othello* or in *Hamlet*. It is true that we cannot sympathize with Antony as we can with Othello or Hamlet, still less with Cleopatra, but for consummate mastery in tragedy, this play bears the palm. The man who can understand and read the last part of this drama

and not be affected by it, does not live, or, if he
lives, we do not envy him. A possible prototype
for Cleopatra is perhaps to be found in the lady
addressed in the following sonnet:

O, from what power hast thou this powerful might
With insufficiency my heart to sway?
To make me give the lie to my true sight,
And swear that brightness doth not grace the day?
Whence hast thou this becoming of things ill,
That in the very refuse of thy deeds
There is such strength and warrantise of skill,
That, in my mind, thy worst all best exceeds?
Who taught thee how to make me love thee more,
The more I hear and see just cause of hate?
O, though I love what others do abhor,
With others thou shouldst not abhor my state:
    If thy unworthiness raised love in me,
    More worthy I to be beloved of thee.
                     Sonnet CL.

Mary Fytton, in her appearance in her statue,
in what we know of her life, and, as far as our
knowledge extends, and it is considerable, in her
characteristics, closely resembles this lady and in
no way differs from her, unless we rely upon the
incorrectly inscribed portrait claimed to be of her
at Arbury. Sir William Knollys, Mary's lover, as
we shall see further on, would have approved of
every word in this sonnet as a description of her.
In looking at the statue, the words arise in the

memory, "Where's my serpent of old Nile?" for
the type is there, permanent in stone. The play
might be called "Cleopatra," for she is by far the
leading character in the play. If we entertain the
speculation that Antony's ruin by Cleopatra should
find its origin in Shakspeare's ruin at Court by
Mary Fytton, we base conjecture on conjecture,
and a speculation, though not wholly devoid of
basis, it must remain.

Several identifications of the lady of the sonnets,
other than with Mary Fytton, have been made
recently, for instance, with Mrs. Davenant of
Oxford, Mrs. Field of London, a Moorish hostess in
Southwark, or the goddess Fortuna, and there is
always in the background the theory that we have
no record or remembrance of her at all. Serious
evidence to support any one of these identifications
seems not yet to have been put forward. It is not
surprising that it should be difficult to identify the
lady to whom the "Dark Lady" sonnets were addressed. After three centuries, or after only a few
years had passed, a love-affair or intrigue, which
did not result in marriage, and which was kept
from public attention, would not usually leave
many traces. Beyond the sonnets themselves,
which were not intended for circulation, the record
consists only of scattered fragments of evidence,

and these must be studied together if we would have any probable theory as to who the lady was.

Sonnet CLII, the last sonnet of the "Dark Lady" series, as they appear in the Quarto, has in its third line a statement which is apparently inapplicable to a young, unmarried woman.

In loving thee thou know'st I am forsworn,
But thou art twice forsworn, to me love swearing;
In act thy bed-vow broke, and new faith torn,
In vowing new hate after new love bearing.
But why of two oaths' breach do I accuse thee,
When I break twenty! I am perjured most;
For all my vows are oaths but to misuse thee,
And all my honest faith in thee is lost.

The answer to this difficulty is a strong confirmation of the theory that Mary Fytton was the lady so unmeasuredly reproached. The words seem to be an allusion to Mary Fytton's exact status in respect to her marriage engagements at the moment. She had on her hands, as the records seem to show, two existing engagements to marry. In Lord Salisbury's Calendar of Manuscripts occurs a letter written by Sir Edward Fytton, Mary's father, to Sir Robert Cecil, the Secretary of State, asking his intervention in a question arisen between Sir Edward and the Vice-Treasurer of Ireland. It seems from the letter that a marriage portion for Mary had at some time been lodged with Sir Henry Wallop, the then Vice-Treasurer, and that its return was now requested, but that the request had been evaded by Sir Henry Wallop's son and successor in office, Henry Wallop, on the ground that Sir Edward's or Mary's acquittance would not be sufficient. It may be taken that the Vice-Treasurer feared that the once intended bridegroom might still come forward and press his claim for it. Mary, very likely, had been married, as was her sister, Anne, in childhood, and the match afterwards disapproved and put aside. The letter, in the abbreviated but substantially complete form in which it has been given to the public, reads (*Hist. MSS. Com.*, Salis. MSS., Part 10, p. 18):

Good Mr. Secretary, help my daughter to her portion, which has been so long in Sir Henry Wallop's hands. If you would send for Mr. Wallop and ask whether he has not good discharge for the same and such as Mr. Treasurer, his father, himself desired, you would see his evasions; without this my poor daughter will be much hindered; wherefore I commend her cause to your protection.

Gawsworth, Jan. 29 [*1600*].

The letter appears in its original form in Mr. Tyler's edition of the sonnets (p. 86), with the date, January 29, 1599, and the original letter is so en-

dorsed, but the endorsement meant, at the time
when it was made, and as it would be written at
present, January 29, 1600. As Sir Henry Wallop,
long time Vice-Treasurer, died in office, April 14,
1599, and was directly succeeded in office by his
son, Henry Wallop, and as this change in office is
referred to in the letter, the date of the letter, as
endorsed, must be January 29, 1599–1600, that is,
January 29, 1600, according to our present system
for the commencement of the year. The letter is
dated by Sir Edward only January 29th. His
omission of the year is not very material, however,
as the following, second, letter is fully dated in
1600. As the sonnet in question was probably
written in or just before 1599, the year in which
Sonnet CXLIV was published, this engagement or
marriage, when the sonnet was written, was still in
existence, and the bridegroom probably still living,
for a difficulty could in 1600 be made, as appears
by the letter, about cancelling the financial arrangement. This still pending matrimonial engagement may then account for the poet's bitter
and angry reproof, "In act thy bed-vow broke."
It seems clear that the phrase, "In act thy bed-vow
broke," implies a limitation, and this qualification
of the broken vow corresponds with Mary's situation, for while the vow was broken in act, it was

still broken in respect to an inchoate and incomplete childhood's contract only, which had not attained the full estate of marriage, and also could be put aside and broken off if it proved desirable to do so. There is a further letter in Lord Salisbury's collection from Sir Edward Fytton to Sir Robert Cecil, of August 5, 1600, in which the negotiation or the dispute as to the dowry is described probably as in course of settlement (*ibid.*, p. 265):

I find by my daughter how much I am maligned by some of whom I have far better deserved; . . . if I prove not innocent of all devices, gain or deceits, even so far as my dearest have thought me too friendly with them that deal now thus with me, let me be disgraced. But I account myself most happy to be heard before your Honours, . . . My daughter in her love writes she wishes my present attendance to purge myself; but I hold it more fit to be sure to meet my accuser face to face, where I hope my innocency shall free me, and therefore I will stay until I may know your pleasure whether I shall come until my adversary be present. I have sent up my bills, wherein Sir Henry Wallop stands in debt to me in £1200, which I have assigned to my daughter Mary, and by direction have sent them into Ireland, there to have them viewed and allowed by the Commissioners lately there, to the end they might have all their dues, as is by your Honours ordered. I now beseech you to stand good to her, and further that Sir Henry Wallop may give her her due.

Gawsworth, 5 August, 1600.

Henry Wallop seems to have been recently knighted; he was probably one among the numerous knights made by Essex during the Irish campaign of 1599 (Chamberlain's Letters, *Camden Society*, notes, pp. 5 and 60); that he was called "Mr. Wallop" in the letter of January 29, 1600, was perhaps an oversight of Sir Edward's. What was the final termination of the dispute has not been brought to light—it was probably settled out of Court in the succeeding year of public scandal—but it is abundantly clear that there was a matrimonial entanglement of Mary's which might account for one of the broken oaths of the sonnet.

An explanation of the second oath-breach referred to in the sonnet is made possible for us by Lady Newdegate's publication of the letters of the Fytton family, the letters written to Anne (Fytton), Lady Newdigate, the sister of Mary. The young lady's permitted, but scarcely permissible, relation to her quasi-parental, married admirer, Sir William Knollys—which is touched on further on in this Note—being considered, it is only necessary to admit, and it seems quite clear, that she, before the sonnet was written, had more or less pledged herself to him, to interpret the phrase in the sonnet, "and new faith torn," as meaning this second engagement, which the poet charged her with hav-

ing contracted and then broken. The "vowing
new hate" might well apply to the elderly and
married lover, for it meets his pretensions exactly.
The old hate, which is implied in the phrase "new
hate," will mean her first dislike to his advances;
the "new love bearing" will refer to the inception
of her engagement to Sir William. The word
"faith," it may be observed, is curiously accurate
in its application to the relation between Mary and
Sir William. Her "two oaths' breach" then would
mean her breaking both her earlier and her later
engagement, which were coexistent, under the
stress of her attachment to the poet, as it is represented in the sonnets. Lord Herbert's growing influence, independently of that of Shakspeare, upon
her attitude toward Sir William, her hate or her
acceptance, should, however, be kept in mind in
reading and interpreting the sonnet, and especially
in understanding the towering passion in which
Shakspeare seems to have written it. This is not
inconsistent with his attitude toward Lord Herbert
at other times, whose power and position he, of
necessity, courted (Sonnet XLI); at this time he
expressed his anger. Lord Herbert's connection
with her attitude toward Sir William is probable, as
Sir William's position appears to have improved
during the future Earl's absence from Court from

November, 1599, to March, 1600. If this view of
the sonnet is taken as accurate, there must have
been such a degree of "faith" established between
Mary and Sir William as early as 1599, or perhaps
a little earlier, as to give a basis for Shakspeare's
charge of breach of faith, and this condition of
"faith" seems to have existed, according to the
passages from Sir William's letters given below.
The elements do not exist for precisely dating the
sonnet within a number of months; the earlier part
of 1599 seems to be the more probable time for it.
A paraphrase of the third and fourth lines of the
sonnet would, upon this theory of them, be: Thy
bed-vow to thy still contracted husband broken in
act, and thy new faith to old Sir William torn,
torn in vowing to me a renewal of thy hate of him,
and after bearing to him thy new love.

It is true that Sir William does not, in his letters,
assert in terms any contract entered into by the
young lady in respect to him, but it is not probable,
on the other hand, that the engagement either was,
or could be, anything but a loose pledge, subjecting
him to the anxiety which he seems throughout to
have felt, according to his letters, and also it is not
likely, in view of his position as a married man,
that he would be explicit on paper as to the terms
of his engagement. As to what he does write,

which is more than frank as to his wishes, he refers to the advisability of "crying silence," and in a letter written in a moment of happiness, he expresses a preference for oral communications. In the last of his letters quoted in this Note, an understanding, such as it was, seems to be unmistakably implied, and as clearly as was allowed by his uncertain position, especially the words, "but both she and I must have patience, and that will bring peace at the last." The whole correspondence of agitations and fears should be studied, particularly Sir William's attitude of hesitation and the lady's coolness, even after the catastrophe, and also his last words, "but I am pleased since she will have it so."

It cannot be doubted that there is at least some reason for the prevalent impression, as it appears in the books, that the "Dark Lady" was Mary Fytton. If, by the light of what little information we have, we can so interpret the phrases of the sonnet as to produce an exact and well-supported explanation of them, we have done all that can be done in a complex of courtship which is now so remote, and which was probably, even at the time, fully understood by very few people.

It must be remembered that Lord Herbert was for less than three years at the Court of Queen

Elizabeth, and although he may have had in that time, besides his affair with Mary Fytton, another with an unknown lady, one in which he displaced Shakspeare, and which is recorded in the sonnets, the general probabilities are much against such a display of energy, and it would take some evidence to establish it, evidence which is not at all forth-coming. There is evidence of one lady who pursued Lord Herbert, and was pursued by him, during that time, and if Mary Fytton, who was that lady, can be connected, as she appears somewhat to be, with the lady of the sonnets, the probability that Lord Herbert and Mary Fytton are the two leading persons mentioned by Shakspeare in the "Dark Lady" sonnets is certainly very decided.

THE FYTTON LETTERS

A point still remains which has been already al-luded to and is of some weight, based upon the cotemporary correspondence in the Fytton Letters. Mistress Mary Fytton, on first arriving at Court as a young Maid of Honour, she was then seventeen years old, was provided with a powerful friend there. Sir William Knollys, a friend of her father's, seems to have undertaken to advise and watch over her, promising his sword in her defense; he was prominent at the Court, a cousin once removed of the Queen's on her mother's side, uncle to the Earl of Essex, joint Lieutenant of Oxfordshire and Berkshire in which counties he had possessions, and at that time the incumbent of the office of Comptroller of the Royal Household, later on its Treasurer, at last becoming Earl of Banbury. Sir William was fifty years old and over when he offered his services in Mary's behalf, and also a married man; his wife was Dorothy, widow of Edmund Brydges, Lord Chandos, an heiress, and older even than Sir William. His advisory office toward the young lady, however, was changed into a persevering love-suit to her, limited as it was by the continued existence of his wife, and he confided his passion to Mary's sister, in a series of letters, undated but paralleling Mary's career, and which, from the unusual circumstances in which they were written, and their bearing upon the controversy as to Mary Fytton, are highly interesting. The sister was Anne, Mrs. Newdigate, of whose husband Sir William was a connection. As having a wife of his own, his letters are, for the most part, rather general than specific, and even to this correspondent, Mary's sister, he is silent, at least in his correspondence, as to his definite proposals, the extent of their acceptance, and their appropriate provisos and limitations. He writes in one of the earlier letters:

Honorable La. As God hath blessed you with encrease, so blessed be you ever & ffreed ffrom all dyscontents, & though myself can not but be now uppon the stage & playe hys part who ys [is] cloyed with to much & yeat readye to starve ffor hunger, My eyes see what I can not attayne to, my eares heare what I doe scant beleve, & my thoughtes are caryed with contrarye conceipts, My hopes are myxt with dispayre & my desyres starved with expectation, but wear [were] my enjoying assured, I could willinglye endure purgatorye ffor a season to purchase my heaven at the last. But the short warning, the distemperature off my head by reason off the toothake, & your syster's going to bed without bydding me godnight, will joyne in one to be a meanes that ffor this tyme I will onlye troble you with these ffew lynes skribled in hast, and wishing you all happynes, a good delyverye off your burden, and your syster in the same case justiffyable, I leave you to God's good protectyon, myself to your dearest syster's true love, & hyr [her] to a constant resolution to love hym onlye who cannot but ever love hyr best, and thus with my best salutations I will ever remayne
Your most assured ffrend,
I would fayne saye brother,
W. KNOLLYS.

The phrases "your sister in the same case justifiable," plainly referring to Mrs. Newdigate's expected maternity, and afterwards, "to love him only," as also, "my ears hear what I do scant believe, and my thoughts are carried with contrary conceits," are worth considerable attention, as they were evidently written early in 1598, the year when, probably in June, Lord Herbert came first to the Court. (*Hist. MSS. Com.*, Salis., Part 8, p. 219.) Mrs. Newdigate's eldest daughter and first child was born May 7, 1598. None other was born until 1600, and in the interval letters, evidently later in the series, were written. The third letter here quoted, that referring to the succeeding baptism of Mrs. Newdigate's eldest child and daughter, was written probably in May or June, 1598. If the letter containing the phrases quoted really precedes the third letter in date, as it precedes it in the order in which the letters are published in the Fytton Letters, and it appears on all accounts to be in its proper place there, it refers to occurrences not connected with Lord Herbert. The reader may compare with these expressions of Sir William's, other expressions in sonnets believed by us to have been written late in 1598 and in 1599, CXII and CXIX, and addressed to Lord Southampton after his return from France. The point has a considerable bearing upon the question at issue in this Note. Perhaps the safe deduction from this evidence, and one more cautious, if we join to it Shakspeare's condemnation: "The more I hear and see just cause of hate," CL, 10, is that Mary was unusually given to questionable and reckless flirtation, but the evidence in any case accords with Shakspeare's criticism of the "Dark Lady." Sir William's allusion to the stage has a curious aptness for the theory that Mary had been attracted by one of the comedians, as his words were written before Lord Herbert arrived at the Court, and before the poet's interest in the lady could have been interfered with by that nobleman. The lady's perhaps abrupt departure for the night, without bidding good-night to her quasi guardian and admirer, will recall to the reader the old "hate," or dislike, implied in Sonnet CLII, 4. Mary's power as an enchantress seems to be plain. "Short warning" perhaps refers to a chance conveyer of the missive. A following letter, as they succeed each other among the Fytton Letters, is, the spelling being, for readier reading, altered into that of the present day:

Honorable sister (I cannot choose but call you so; because I desire nothing more than to have it so): Your fair written letter, and more fairly indited,

I have received and read more than once or twice, seeking to find there which so much you endeavour to put me in hope of. It is true that Winter's cold is the murderer of all good fruits, in which climate I dwell, and do account it as a purgatory allotted to me for my many offences committed against the Highest, the rather because I am more observant and devoted unto his creature than to himself, from which to be delivered, since there is no means but the devout prayers and orisons of my good friends, let me entreat your fair self to pierce the heavens with your earnest and best prayers to the Effecter and Worker of all things for my delivery, and that once I may be so happy as to feel the pleasing comfort of a delightful Summer, which I doubt not will yield me the deserved fruit of my constant desires, which as yet no sooner bud by the heat of the morning sun but they are blasted by an untimely frost, so as in the midst of my best comforts I see nothing but dark despair. I could complain of Fortune which led me blindly into this barren desert where I am ready to starve for want of my desired food, and of myself that would suffer my reason to be betrayed by my will in following so blind a guide. But to all my wounds I will apply your plaster, which is patience, a virtue I must needs confess, but having in a sort lost her force because it is forced. Continue, I earnestly entreat you, your prayer for my delivery, and your best means for my obtaining that without the which I am not myself, having already given my best part to one whose I am more than mine own. But I must cry silence, lest I speak too loud, committing this secret only to yourself, to whom as I wish all happiness and your own heart's desire, so I will ever remain

Your most affectionate brother,
W. KNOWLESS THAN I WOULD.

It seems that Mary had fairly fascinated her elderly suitor; the "Winter's cold" was doubtless the lady's coldness rather than his existing marriage, and the "frost" was a part of the same climatic misfortune. In his last sentence the suitor seems to be impressed by the necessity of keeping a certain degree of silence, considering his already married state, while his correspondent decidedly encouraged him in his suit. The words "dark despair" seem to refer to alternations of favour and chilliness, and the witticism of his signature is not equalled every day.

Sir William became godfather to Anne Newdigate's first child in 1598, and was represented at the ceremony of baptism by Sir Christopher Blount, his brother-in-law, Sir William being not present in person. He writes in his letter of acceptance:

. . . but such is my bondage to this place as I have neither liberty to please myself nor satisfy my good friends' expectation, amongst which I must account you in the foremost rank, as well for your own worthiness as for being so nearly united both in nature and love to those which I honour much, and who may

more command me than all the world besides. But
my thoughts of that party I will leave to be discovered,
not by this base means of pen and paper, but by myself.
Accept, I pray you, of my lawful excuse for not coming
myself, assuring you that I will be ever ready to perform any friendly duty to you; I have entreated my
brother, Blunt, to supply my place in making your
little one a Christian soul, and give it what name it
shall please you. Imagine what name I love best, and
that do I nominate, but refer the choice to yourself,
and if I might be as happy to·be a father as a godfather
I would think myself exceeding rich, but that will
never be until one of your own tribe be a party player.
, . .

The position of Sir William in his love-suit was
most difficult, as he was not able to propose a
present marriage. His words and his manner in
writing of Mary in this letter are those of an
encouraged though but a prospective lover; he
doubtless thought that he could arrive at an understanding which perhaps became established, so far
as, in the nature of the case, any certain assurance
was possible, between this and the succeeding letter,
written much later, perhaps a year and a half, or
nearly so. The child, in accordance with Sir
William's wish, and no doubt with Mrs. Newdigate's wish, was named Mary; he also advised
Mrs. Newdigate as to the proper manner of the
nursing of her child. He therefore seems to have

stood at this time on decidedly intimate terms with the family. Notwithstanding this tendency to closer relations, however, and his tentative success, which seems to have been allowed by the lady's family, and although he may have confided to them some sort of acceptance of his proposals, still the lady would not have readily given an unqualified acceptance, which would have at once limited and compromised her, and it is probable therefore that no positive letter to that effect was ever written by him. The succeeding letter contains a reference to his nephew, the Earl of Essex, and his political overthrow:

Fair Gossip, I must crave pardon for my so long silence, not grown by a negligent forgetfulness of so good a friend, but forced by a distraction I have had concerning the Noble Earl of Essex, which hath made me careless to satisfy myself or my friends. I leave to you to imagine the discomforts I take hereof, when your sister is fain to blame me for my melancholy and small respect of her who, when I am myself, is the only comfort of my heart. She is now well, and hath not been troubled with the mother [hysteria] of a long time. I would God I might as lawfully make her a mother as you are; I would be near both at Arbury to shun the many griefs which this place affordeth, and she should enjoy the company of the most loving and kind sister that ever I knew. My heart is so full of sorrow at this time for my Lord of Essex being dangerously sick before his restraint as I am scant myself. . .

The letter shows Mary at this time requiring
"respect" or attentions from Sir William, who
thinks her "the only comfort of my heart," and
it can be surely inferred that that anomalous relation toward her, a quasi acceptance as a suitor
was established, and had continued for some length
of time. He was a conquest worth retaining, and
still had no claim on her. Possibly she had found
more security with Lord Herbert by favouring
Sir William. When this letter was written, Lord
Herbert had just left, or was about to leave, the
Court. As the Earl of Essex' illness under his
censure and detention began in October, 1599
(*Sidney Papers*, Whyte to Sidney, Oct. 25 and Nov.
4, 1599), he even proposing to make his Will, the
letter was written probably not very long afterwards. Lord Herbert left the Court November
29, 1599, remaining away for three months and
more. Sir William's commendation of Anne as a
loving and kind sister is in keeping with what appears of her in respect to Mary later in life, and his
reference to hysteria will be noted, in this connection, with due appreciation. The allusion to his
nearness to Arbury refers, of course, to his lands
in Oxfordshire and Berkshire, of which counties
he was then joint Lieutenant, and later on Lord
Lieutenant. He writes again:

. . . The best news I can send you is that your sister is in good health and going to the Court within two or three days, though I think she could be better pleased to be with her best sister upon some conditions. Her greatest fear is that while the grass groweth the horse may starve, and she thinketh a bird in the bush is worth two in the hand. [*sic*.] But both she and I must have patience, and that will bring peace at the last. Thus, in some haste, with my best salutations to yourself, and my kindest blessing to my daughter, I wish you your heart's desire, and will remain ever

Your faithful friend and gossip

W. KNOLLYS.

The references in this letter to a more or less complete understanding between Sir William and Mary are quite unmistakable. The inversion of the proverb, "A bird in the hand," etc., is notable, and much as if Mary's chase after a difficult prize, it may be thought, Lord Herbert, had been observed by Sir William and bluntly commented on. She maintained this pursuit, or so Sir William suspected, notwithstanding her acceptance of him. The reader will compare, as to Mary's attitude in this matter, Sonnet CXLIII; the parallel is, to say the least of it, striking, for the resemblance of the simile in the sonnet and in the letter suggests with much probability that it may have been common in the current talk of the time. The "feathered creature" is Lord Herbert, as we think. Lord Herbert, when this letter was written, was most probably on the eve of returning to Court. The letter and the sonnet are not cotemporary; the sonnet probably preceded the letter by a little over a year. The proverb as to the grass growing, with the words, "Her greatest fear," refer, of course, to Sir William's existing marriage, and Mary's hesitation as to committing her prospects in that uncertain direction. The proverb, it will be remembered, is mentioned by Hamlet (III, ii, 358). So also, by the way, Ophelia mentions pansies, the Fyttons' flower, "that's for thoughts," the next words being, "A document [instruction] in madness; thoughts and remembrance fitted," the rosemary being for remembrance (IV, v, 176). The word "fitted" has a strange pertinence here, if this theory is true. Sir William's anxious sentence, "But both she and I must have patience," etc., implies, beyond a doubt, that an understanding in some degree had arisen between them, and that the delay worried him. The letter speaks of her return to Court as about to happen, which dates it almost certainly after February 21, 1600, near which date Lady Sidney paid her a visit during her illness in London, as has been noted earlier in this abstract. Sir William also seems to have known of this ill-

13

ness, and to have been more or less present; it was perhaps not very severe. This would date the letter during Lord Herbert's absence from Court, and that young nobleman's illness, when Sir William's suit might advance, as the letter suggests that it had, and when Mary seems to have been well enough to receive him, although she had felt compelled by it to leave the Court. The understanding, however, seems to still date back far enough, when the letter next preceding this is also read, to account for one of the two broken pledges of Sonnet CLII. The letter now commented on, from the allusion to his god-daughter, was probably written before the birth of Anne's second child, May 27, 1600, while the expectation of Mary's return to Court, mentioned in the letter, probably places it rather earlier than May. We can date the letter, most probably, in early March, 1600. There are also two letters by Sir William doubting his success, and one evincing a degree of distress; the allusion to them is all that is necessary here.

How exact seems to be Shakspeare's reference to him in these lines:

Whoever hath her wish, thou hast thy "Will,"
And "Will" to boot, and "Will" in overplus;
Sonnet CXXXV, 1.

The elderly Sir William might well be called a surplusage among Mary's lovers.   In an article which appeared in the *Fortnightly Review* immediately after the publication of the Fytton Letters (Mr. William Archer in *The Case against Southampton*, December, 1897, p. 819), this evidence was considered as almost conclusive that the third "William" of the sonnet "appears manifestly in the person of Sir William himself," and it appears to us also as though the point were a very strong one.   The allusion exactly suits him, and as there are three men named William mentioned in the sonnet, this Sir William supplies the third, the other two being Lord William Herbert and William Shakspeare, a solution which would quiet not a few doubts as to the persons referred to in these sonnets if it could be admitted as conclusive.

There is also the even stronger point that Shakspeare and the dedicatee of Sonnets XXXV, XL, and other sonnets of the sort, were lovers of the same lady, and if Lord Herbert is accepted as the dedicatee of those sonnets, the indications, especially from his character and the character and probable date of those sonnets, much favouring that dedication, it is all but inevitable that Mary. Fytton was the lady, there being no doubt as to his relation to her.   Their relation, and the central date, 1599, established by *The Passionate Pilgrim*, together with the other fragmentary evidence, here noted, go very far to establishing them as two of the personages in the drama of Shakspeare's sonnets. If Lord Herbert is accepted, Mary Fytton must almost certainly be accepted also, and, if the lady is accepted, so must Lord Herbert with her.

Further, it cannot be doubted that there is an intrinsic likeness between the passage from *Love's Labour's Lost* (IV, iii, 258), added for Court performance, probably in 1597, and Sonnet CXXVII and their concurrence in date is certainly probable also. Adding to this indication the circumstance that Mary Fytton was then at the Court, and the decided resemblance between the characters of Rosaline, of the "Dark Lady" and of Mary Fytton, and also the probable allusion to Mary's name in Sonnet CLI, the probable allusion to her age in the version in *The Passionate Pilgrim* of Sonnet CXXXVIII, and the markedly probable allusion to her matrimonial engagements in Sonnet CLII, also the similarity of the characteristics of the "Dark Lady" of the sonnets to the description, as far as it goes, of Mary Fytton in the letters of Sir William Knollys, the nearly certain concurrence of the date of these sonnets with the date of Sir

William's letters, and his seeming appearance twice in the sonnets (CXXXV, CLII), also her certain acquaintance with and seemingly observed pursuit of Lord Herbert, the nearly certain concurrence of the date of the "Dark Lady" sonnets with the time of that acquaintance, and the probable allusions to him in Sonnets CXLIII, XL, XLI, CXXXIV and elsewhere, we have a chain of evidence which, though not rising to strict proof, is still so consistent as, taken together, to lead us to choose Mary Fytton as the all but proved original of the "Dark Lady" of Shakspeare's sonnets.

The tendency of the evidence is toward the conclusion that Mary Fytton, Rosaline and the Lady of the Sonnet, Shakspeare's love and Lord Herbert's rejected mistress, were all the same lady, and it is clearly more probable that Mary Fytton was the original of the "Dark Lady" than that she was not. The reader will judge for himself, on the evidence, which is not inconsiderable, whether this uncontrollable passion of the great poet's was given to one of the most fascinating and forward ladies of the Court, or, as is less likely, especially when we consider the description which is given of the lady in the sonnets, to some lady less distinguished or unknown.

Lightning Source UK Ltd.
Milton Keynes UK
UKHW021107090119
335176UK00013B/1541/P